MAXIMIZING EMPLOYEE PRODUCTIVITY

A Manager's Guide

Robert E. Sibson

MAXIMIZING EMPLOYEE PRODUCTIVITY

A Manager's Guide

American Management Association

New York • Atlanta • Boston • Chicago • Kansas City • San Francisco • Washington, D. C.
Brussels • Mexico City • Tokyo • Toronto

This publication is designed to provide accurate and authoritative information in regard to the subject matter covered. It is sold with the understanding that the publisher is not engaged in rendering legal, accounting, or other professional service. If legal advice or other expert assistance is required, the services of a competent professional person should be sought.

Library of Congress Cataloging-in-Publication Data

Sibson, Robert Earl, 1925–
    Maximizing employee productivity : a managers guide / Robert E. Sibson.
        p.   cm.
    Includes bibliographical references and index.
    ISBN 0-8144-5094-6
    1. Personnel management.   2. Labor productivity.   I Title.
HF5549.S58534   1994
658.3'14—dc20   93-41638
                                                                 CIP

Printing number

10   9   8   7   6   5   4   3   2   1

Contents

v

Preface

I have worked with companies on productivity issues for more than thirty years, and it's time to write another book on the subject.

I conducted my first productivity study in 1962 for the Federal Reserve Bank of Philadelphia. In the early 1970s, I had a client assignment to study the views and practices relating to employee productivity in over 300 companies. At that time I also had my consulting associates at Sibson & Company make a comprehensive review of all published material. That material became the basis for my first book on productivity, *Increasing Employee Productivity*, which was published by AMACOM* in 1976. This was also the first book to be published about productivity. A lot has changed since then, and business has learned more about productivity management. It is clearly time for a new book on increasing employee productivity.

One thing has not changed. After thirty years and many experiences, I still think that specific productivity programs should be tailored to each organization.

This book presents a general method of productivity management, which I call the EP process—for "employee productivity." This general method can be customized for any organization to increase employee productivity. The material in this book is based mostly on my consulting experiences. I have never counted as-

*Robert E. Sibson, *Increasing Employee Productivity*, American Management Association, New York, 1976.

signments by subject, because so much of my work has been for clients I advised in all areas of human resources, including productivity management, and because a lot of functional human resources issues involve productivity questions. However, I guess that I had well over 100 client cases relating to productivity management between 1976 and 1987, when I stopped doing project consulting work. Many of the company cases and examples in this book were clients for whom I did productivity consulting.

In 1976 I started holding three-day conferences in Florida, and information from some of these added substantially to the information and experience base for this book. Two of these conferences each year for a ten-year period focused on employee productivity. These conferences were by invitation only and were attended by high-level professionals. The attendance was limited in each session to a maximum of fifteen persons in order to get detailed case information. These conferences probably added another hundred cases of experience in the area of productivity management.

That is a very broad experience base, one that I hope deserves your attention. In addition, the material for this book came from three other sources:

1. Since 1975, employee productivity has been the subject of about three dozen sections in *The Sibson Report*. Each of these sections required gathering fresh information and experiences.
2. Since 1987, I have done only network consulting by telephone and by mail. This work is directed at specific questions, and many of these network consulting assignments involved productivity.
3. In the spring of 1992, I ran a survey of 200 companies to get updated information on company thinking and experience on productivity. That material was also very helpful, particularly with respect to the recent experiences of many companies with various productivity programs. The results of this survey are reported in Appendix A.

These were the basic sources of information for this book. The process of productivity management presented here and recommended for your use thus stems from actual work with companies and from hundreds of cases over many years. You may agree or disagree with the recommendations, but you will know that they are based on many success experiences.

Every organization that has used the basic EP approach to productivity management has been successful—every one of them. Of course, I can't prove that, but I say it anyway with the hope that my reputation of thirty-three years as a human resources management consultant, plus the fact that I no longer do project consulting work, will convince you that I think that is correct.

What you will find in this book are recommendations that are very different from those proposed by many productivity enthusiasts. I'm not alone in my views, but many consultants disagree with me, perhaps because the EP method of increasing productivity does not require the use of consultants.

This book presents a commonsense, practical business approach to productivity management. The process uses sound management practices.

Managers won't find strange words or some cult of behavior in the process recommended. This process uses proven management practices. This is a manager's approach to increasing productivity.

When you write a book, it's a good idea to have a specific audience in mind. This is helpful even though the author hopes that others with different backgrounds will be interested in the book also. The target audience for this book is operating managers, particularly operating managers who manage between 50 and 500 employees. Although some of the actions I recommend can be taken only by senior executives, most are applicable to managers at any level. Human resources professionals should also find much useful information in this book.

You may not find this book as entertaining as some others. I am a consultant, not a novelist or an entertainer. Productivity is serious business and needs to be treated that way. If you are looking for something resembling quality circles or total quality management, you won't find it in this book. QC is mostly history, and I believe TQM will probably be the same by the end of the decade.

What you *will* find are specific recommendations for increasing employee productivity. With this book you can do effective productivity management work without hiring me or any other consultant.

When you have written as many books as I have, you have dedicated books to a lot of people. The 1976 productivity book was dedicated to our boys—Jay and Rick—and, of course, we love them still. But each book should have a new dedication. So this book is dedicated to our grandchildren, Nicolas, Natalie, and Marie—and to your grandchildren. All of our grandchildren will somehow have to pay off the enormous debt we have piled up for them, mostly since 1976.

If we continue to pile up the national debt in the next sixteen years as we have in the last sixteen years, the interest on that debt alone will exceed our entire national income. So we must deal with the national debt and can do so only by responsible actions from Congress or by managers increasing productivity. We have no choice—we must increase productivity.

Robert E. Sibson

1

The Productivity Opportunity

You must have an interest in productivity, or you wouldn't have picked up this book. I hope you have become a productivity evangelist by the time you are finished reading it.

The United States is facing great economic problems. Improving productivity is the best opportunity that exists for dealing with these national economic issues.

Many companies are facing severe problems of competitiveness and restructuring. Productivity management is a major opportunity for dealing with these problems. In fact, there is an opportunity for many companies to have, as a basic business strategy, a substantial business improvement through greater employee productivity. Within all types of organizations there are similar opportunities to improve operational results by increased employee productivity. Many people could improve their positions and their career opportunities by increasing their effectiveness, by improving their own personal productivity.

Some say that lagging productivity is a great problem. I say that improving productivity is a great opportunity. Both statements say the same thing. But by emphasizing the opportunities, considerations become answer-oriented instead of grief-oriented. A positive focus on productivity also highlights the fact that we now have a special opportunity to increase productivity much more than has ever been achieved in the past and that there are commonsense methods to exploit this special opportunity.

This Special Opportunity

Increasing employee productivity is the single most important economic issue in the United States. If we don't improve productivity a lot more in the next decade than we have in the recent past, ours will likely be a second-rate economic nation by the twenty-first century.

When Don Regan was chief executive officer of Merrill Lynch, he would spend a few days from time to time at his winter home in John's Island, near Vero Beach, Florida, which was right around the corner from where we lived. Sometimes the two of us would play a quick game of golf. We never talked business; he came to Florida to get away from it. But one day I did ask him what he thought was the most important single issue in American business. He shot right back, "Productivity!" Then after a few thoughtful moments, he added, "If we increase productivity enough, we can afford to pay whatever is necessary to solve the other problems, whatever they are." That says it all in a very few words. That conversation led me to become seriously involved in productivity management work again.

In a recent speech in Vero Beach, Bill Seidman, formerly head of the RTC and the FDIC, pointed out that the difference between a 1 percent increase in national productivity and a 3 percent national gain in productivity was the difference between misery on the one hand and a balanced budget on the other. His point related to the consequences of a continuing increase in the national debt, but the important thing to me was that productivity was key to the national welfare.

We now have a special opportunity to increase productivity. Since the early 1980s we have had an opportunity to increase productivity by 4 to 6 percent a year for at least twenty years. This potential for greater effectiveness of work is mostly technology-based and will continue into the twenty-first century. The effect of an improvement in productivity of up to 6 percent a year on the standard of living is mind-boggling. Twenty years from now it is quite possible that living standards could be more than double what they are today. The family incomes of the lowest-paid, full-time workers could be about equal to the average income for all workers today, net of inflation. No full-time worker would live below the poverty threshold.

Nationally, a productivity increase of 4 to 6 percent a year for twenty years would not only double living standards, but it would balance the budget, eliminate the national debt, and pay for every social program discussed before Congress so far. Those are the potential benefits from this special opportunity to increase productivity. This is the productivity dividend.

At the company level, a 4 to 6 percent improvement in productivity could double the income of employees and, at the same time, the profits of many businesses could increase four-fold. To get an appreciation of the impact of a 4 to 6 percent increase in productivity, think of the lifestyles that existed one hundred years ago and how much better our material condition is today than it was in the 1890s. Extrapolate that into the future at two to three times the rate of the improvement of the past. Then before the year 2020, standards of living can be as much greater, compared to today, as the living standards of today are compared to the living standards of the early 1890s.

The potential for a 4 to 6 percent productivity gain is an average productivity improvement opportunity for the entire country and for all organizations. Some organizations and some individuals won't improve productivity at all, but others can experience up to a 10 percent productivity gain each year, perhaps for twenty years. Some companies have already experienced that rate of productivity improvement.

Historically, productivity improvement has resulted from capital substitution, and that is what will mostly happen in the future, but at a much higher rate. Because of technological advances, we are at a point in time where there is a massive substitution of equipment for human effort throughout the country. It is difficult to comprehend the extent to which machines might substitute for human effort, let alone quantify the opportunities. A 4 to 6 percent a year increase in productivity for twenty years may prove to be *conservative*, or we may fall on our economic faces and miss this incredible opportunity to increase productivity.

No one can be sure that this great leap forward in productivity is going to happen for one business or for our nation. Information on the rate of machine substitution just proves that it *could* happen.

There has never been a better opportunity for greater increases in productivity for an extended period of time than currently exists. This is because of three main factors: (1) unprecedented opportunities for capital substitution, (2) the application of basic new technologies, and (3) increases in the output of work that are less limited.

There are a number of reasons why there are such great opportunities for capital substitution. The new equipment (mostly computers, related equipment, and software) is relatively cheap compared to labor. The cost of the capital is getting cheaper while labor costs continue to increase. These new machines are general purpose, which means they become obsolete very slowly. Most computers and related equipment are easy to move or access from great distances, and that also makes these machines more immune from obsolescence.

Technology will contribute to forms of capital substitution in many ways in addition to computers and communications technology. Sometimes even scientists have difficulty comprehending the application of new technologies to new products and higher employee productivity. There have been basic scientific breakthroughs in biotechnology, energy, materials, communication systems, and robotics, as well as in computers. In the laboratory, scientists can move particles of matter to create or change materials and, theoretically, they can change water into oil or stones into gold. These breakthroughs are basic, and they may spawn whole new generations of products and services, which, in time, will very likely have a dramatic effect on our ability to increase the effectiveness at work. All of this is in *addition* to the effect of known capital substitution, mostly from computers.

Much of what is "output" in the future will be open-ended, and that also presents a greater opportunity for increasing employee productivity. Until recent years, the numerator of the productivity equation (output) was limited by how much could be sold and used. For example, the number of shoes you could produce was limited by the number of pairs of feet in the world.

As we move into the third leg of our economy, which is

mostly the personal care, leisure, and entertainment businesses, the output is less limited or unlimited. Mental activities such as learning, for example, have no limit that we now understand, and there are some who think that the average life expectancy may become as much as 200 years.

Another reason why the potential for greater output is so unique is because machines now substitute for people's mental as well as their physical effort. Computers don't think yet, but they do count and memorize much better than the human mind. This capability to substitute machinery for mental effort has an enormous potential effect on productivity.

Finally, it is important to recognize that people control more and more of the machines that are being substituted for human effort, whereas, in the past, machinery almost always controlled what people did. People often determine what computers produce, and that means that the use of computers may result in greater work effectiveness or the creation of enormous amounts of unused or useless information produced by informaniacs. Much will depend upon managing people more effectively.

It is conditions such as those described above that make it possible for a truly extraordinary increase in productivity in the United States, in many companies, in many organizational units, and for most workers. Case studies on the amount of investment in the new technologies and the impact of these technologies on productivity have led to the prediction that productivity can increase at an annual rate of 4 to 6 percent for at least twenty years.

Productivity must be managed properly. There must be a proper process for such management. The EP process is the best way to exploit this special opportunity to increase productivity.

I didn't invent the EP process; thousands of managers had to meet very specific problems and develop proper productivity management actions. I have just put their actions together in an understandable fashion, and I describe this process here so you can use it yourself.

To apply the EP process of productivity management, you need to be competent in managing. You also need to know basic things about productivity.

Productivity Briefing

Those who work on productivity management don't have to be productivity experts, but they must understand some of the basics of employee productivity. This section presents, in a random manner, essential information about productivity that should be possessed by all who are involved in productivity work.

Productivity means doing high-quality work with great efficiency. The actual productivity formula today is pretty complicated in some operations, but in essence, productivity still means output per man-hour.

Of course, output must be usable and saleable. That means the output must be of high quality. Total quality management people make a big thing of this, but productivity work has always assumed that output was of sufficient quality to meet customers' expectations.

There are many ways to improve productivity. For example, productivity may improve if work is done a better way, or when work is done by machines more quickly than by humans, or when work is more often done correctly the first time. Most productivity improvement has occurred because machines replaced human effort, which, as stated earlier, will likely continue to be equally true in the future. Managers should have a good understanding of the specific ways in which productivity can be increased in their own operations. The chances are that the list of ways to increase productivity in your operation is very different than it was in the operations I ran, which were mostly consulting firms, a conference business, and a professional publication operation.

Improving productivity doesn't happen automatically; it is not a natural event. *People* determine the level of productivity, and people must work consciously to bring about higher productivity. Productivity gains thus usually require affirmative actions by *people*. Productivity improvement requires correct and productive actions by people.

Greater productivity does not usually mean working harder but more likely means working smarter. Of course, if people are working at low effort levels, then if there is an increase in effort to reasonable levels, productivity will increase. Most worker-initiated productivity improvement, however, results from working smarter, not harder.

For many years, working smarter, not harder, was the slogan of the Johns-Manville Corporation until asbestos litigation caused it to work mostly for survival. The company gave great credit to this simple idea for a great deal of the productivity improvement that occurred there for many years.

Productive work is not necessarily more stressful work. The variables of stress are mostly related to personal traits, the work climate, and the nature of the operations rather than to work excellence. Productivity doesn't correlate very much with the quality of work life or worker satisfaction. There may be higher levels of job satisfaction with higher levels of productivity because most people take pride in their work and genuinely want to do their best. But there may also be high job satisfaction when the work pace is leisurely and productivity is low. For example, a study made at Days Inn showed no correlation between productivity and job satisfaction in more than 200 similar motels. In fact, the level of job satisfaction was about the same in the very high and very low productivity operations. Job satisfaction varied a great deal in the motels in the middle 50 percent of productivity.

Productivity means *change*. With machine substitution and high technology, change can be very dramatic and requires very different practices. Change is always its own form of work, creates challenge, and often causes difficulties for those whose jobs are changed.

For the economy overall, greater productivity will ultimately mean more jobs. Greater productivity makes lower prices possible and adds to higher earnings for workers, which means more sales and more work. However, in one workplace and in the short run, higher productivity often means fewer jobs. That means people are transferred, downgraded, or terminated.

Recognize that the level of productivity is dependent upon three basic variables. (1) Employee productivity is dependent upon a well-educated workforce that possesses a high work ethic and is consistently inclined to do its reasonable best at work. (2) Productivity is dependent upon available capital to substitute for human effort and the ability to finance that capital substitution.

(3) Productivity is dependent upon the effective management of people.

Productivity cannot be an "on-off" activity. From time to time there may be a need for a special emphasis or a new tactic to vitalize productivity management activities. Generally, however, productivity management is best done as a continuing effort and as a regular part of the management process in any organization.

Go for continuous improvement in productivity. If you somehow get a big jump in productivity, that's a dividend, but don't count on it, and don't go for the "big bang." An operation never achieves perfection in productivity, and it isn't usually cost effective to try to get the maximum productivity possible. There is an optimum level of productivity in each type of operation, and managers should have a sense of that optimum level.

Productivity and enterprise success are always linked, although not necessarily in a single year. Higher productivity will always mean greater profitability in a commercial firm in the long run. Productivity and operating unit success or personal success are also usually linked.

Productivity improvement must be *managed*, which is a good reason to call this work productivity management. Greater productivity is not the natural result of human effort. In fact, many productive practices are often unnatural and must be learned.

The government can do a lot to help productivity improvement, but the important productivity actions must be taken at the organizational level. If enough organizations improve productivity substantially, then national productivity will improve also. For example, some time ago I made a major study of "leadership companies." The number one factor found in all companies regarded as leadership companies was high levels of employee productivity.

I was recently involved in a major study by a very large company that wanted to determine the qualities of successful operating managers. Every person thought to be successful as a manager in that company managed a group that had high levels of productivity. This, then, is the ultimate lesson of productivity. Our country, a company, a business unit, and an individual can all benefit from productivity improvement. It is an opportunity for everyone. You could say that increasing productivity is a win-win-win-win situation.

The EP Process of Productivity Management

The process of productivity management that is recommended here has been labeled the EP process of productivity management—EP for "employee productivity." EP might also mean "effective people." It can mean "equipment" and "personnel," which are the resources of productivity management. But EP is mostly just a label to identify this particular approach to productivity management.

This approach is results-oriented, not process-oriented. The steps in the process evolved over the years and are based on a discovery of what worked, what practices actually resulted in higher employee productivity. EP is based, therefore, on the experiences of many managers in hundreds of operations.

The recommended process is also based on American traits and American traditions. Some have erred grievously by copying what was designed (by Americans) to work in Japan. It is not Japan bashing, but just common sense, to urge companies, as I have for the past twenty years, to "increase productivity the American way."

There is no mysticism in EP. You aren't asked to "believe" or wait to get "it." EP involves only familiar, practical, and proven management practices. It is a simple approach to understand. You don't have to hire consultants to guide you in designing and implementing the EP approach in your particular company. That may be one reason why many consultants don't recommend this system.

You don't need a PhD in mathematics or psychology to implement action steps in the EP process of productivity improvement. What you need to know about is management. That is another reason why some gurus don't support the EP system: many of these gurus lack experience in managing.

Because EP involves commonsense management actions, there are no new, time-consuming programs that must be initiated, and there are no fundamental organizational changes. Existing managers take actions. They get support as they need it from existing organizational staff units.

EP is done in manageable steps. It involves continuing efforts in productivity improvement. The commonsense management actions under the EP approach are a part of managing. This isn't a passive approach to productivity management. There are very specific affirmative actions. But all such actions are management actions. The productivity management actions I recommend have a stand-alone value in managing *and* also contribute to greater productivity.

Here, briefly presented, is my recommended EP process for productivity management, step by step. Each of the twelve steps identified here are described in the succeeding twelve chapters. These steps should be considered for implementation in the order of presentation.

Step 1—Get executive commitment: The first action step is to make sure that executives are committed to productivity management. In the EP process, executive commitment basically means they must support and be conscious of productivity improvement work. The executive commitment in the EP process is to work excellence. Executives are not being asked to force any particular practice or system into the organization, or to require a uniform application of any technique.

It is helpful if the executives themselves are productive and if they do productivity management work well with their own direct reports. But that isn't essential in the recommended productivity system. I have yet to meet an executive who didn't want higher productivity, but I have met some who thought that levels of productivity didn't make much of a difference in business results. Many executives doubt that productivity can be improved through the better management of personnel or by any productivity management effort.

Executives don't have to be personally involved in the EP process of productivity. However, they must support productivity management in the four ways outlined.

Step 2—Develop a productivity culture: The second step in the EP process is to develop a productivity consciousness throughout the organization. Every manager must think productivity. Every employee must have a basic effectiveness ethic, or a desire to do his or her reasonable best at work. There must be a constant focus on the effectiveness of work and a persistent striving for excellence. What you are doing is building a productivity *culture* in your company.

The result you are seeking is a lot of continuing initiatives by employees. Doing things more productively becomes part of everyone's job and a part of the employees' mind-set.

Step 3—Make productivity part of every manager's job: Assign the job of productivity management to every manager. Give managers the time to do the job and provide the support they need. Measure managers' performances partly by how well they manage productivity. Reward those managers who increase productivity. Replace those managers who don't manage productivity well.

Only managers should have responsibility and authority for productivity. Human resources professionals, industrial engineers, consultants, and others only assist and advise operating managers under the EP process of productivity management.

Step 4—Measure productivity: To make productivity the job of every worker and manager and to reward performance, there must be productivity measures. Therefore, measuring productivity is an integral part of productivity management and one of the essentials of the EP approach. Establish productivity measures for every organizational unit throughout the company, without exception. Establish performance measures for every person.

If you don't measure productivity, you can't manage productivity. Without productivity measures, you would never know if actions taken to increase effectiveness actually did increase productivity or if they detracted from productivity.

Step 5—Utilize technology: Productivity mostly occurs through capital substitution, and the capital is increasingly worker-controlled. This means that some understanding of the new technologies and the proper utilization of machines such as computers is critical to increasing productivity. Assuring the proper use of worker-controlled equipment is an important part of productivity management.

Step 6—Remove unproductive practices: Early in any organized effort to do productivity work, consider launching a vendetta against unproductive practices of any type everywhere in the organization. When there are unionized employees, removing unproductive practices means productivity bargaining. But don't assume that unproductive practices only exist in union situations. There are many unproductive practices at every level of a company's operation, and a key part of the EP process is to remove unproductive methods and obsolete practices.

Step 7—Empower employees: The delegation of responsibility for productivity improvement should go through management levels to every worker in the company. Productivity improvement is the job of every person. Delegate first to each operating manager, as low in the organization as possible. Then those managers must empower every worker. Make every worker responsible for working as effectively as possible.

Participation or involvement just won't do it. You must empower employees.

Step 8—Utilize networking: Effective networking is a key part of the EP process of managing productivity. Every worker should have access to information and experience that will be helpful in achieving work excellence. I think that networking will be an increasingly important facet of management. Effectiveness will depend a lot on whom is networked and the excellence of the networking process.

Step 9—Ensure excellence in staffing: Put your productivity dollars up front; recruit effective people. Then make sure you use those people in the correct assignments and have them do their work well.

In spite of educational deficiency and pockets of chronic labor scarcity, there is plenty of talent to meet the needs of any organization. However, there must be effectiveness in recruiting and staffing if you are going to consistently recruit highly talented workers.

Step 10—Restructure the operation: Restructuring is an important productivity action step for many companies. Restructuring generally means two things: streamlining and reduction in staff. Organizational streamlining involves eliminating one or more organizational levels. A reduction in staff means reducing the proportional number of staff and support positions. Such actions result in downsizing the workforce and that improves productivity.

Step 11—Manage performance: Logically, if the performance and capability of workers improve, productivity will tend to increase. That's why performance management is a step in the EP process. Performance appraisal and training are key parts of performance management. Training must be continuous and related to improving the effectiveness of work.

Step 12—Reward performance: It is fair to reward greater effectiveness of work. Such rewards give people incentive to increase the effectiveness of their work. The plans and practices to reward for performance exist. What is needed is the will to implement them. Productivity management provides another important reason for rewarding performance.

Applying the Recommended Process

Each step in the recommended EP productivity management process is described in some detail in the next chapters. What is described is productivity management, not a canned program. I list a dozen steps in this book, but you can develop still others. For example, some companies have a greater emphasis on training and education and have that as a separate step. Others believe that team building should be a productivity action step. There is no limit on the number of steps you can use, as long as the action steps result in greater productivity.

You may decide that one or more of the twelve steps prescribed is not relevant in your operation, or that what you are now doing in that area is sufficient. For example, some might think that there is no need to change their staffing practices.

I think that every company and every organizational unit in every company should adopt at least the first four steps that are listed. They are truly the basics of productivity management. They are also the foundation for other productivity management actions. Specifically, then, I recommend that companies proceed first with the four required steps in the process (action steps 1 through 4). The four basic steps in the EP process can be accomplished within three months and at almost zero cash cost. The required time commitment for the first four steps is moderate.

Measure the results from the four steps. Reinvest some of the gain from improved productivity in additional action steps in the EP process. This is an investment-return approach to increasing productivity.

Always do productivity work in manageable steps. Don't proceed further if the steps you take don't provably contribute to greater effectiveness and higher work excellence.

The steps after the basic four are rarely the same in any two companies. Consider operations-related activities first. Look for targets of opportunity and pursue them vigorously. Action steps 5 through 8 are examples of operations-related activities. It is in this second phase where the big payoffs in productivity management work are most likely to occur. Operations-related productivity action steps can proceed for years. It is the operations-related action steps that represent a special opportunity for extraordinary improvement in productivity.

There are also productivity improvement actions that are highly dependent on human resources actions and, therefore, excellence in human resources work. Every company should consider the productivity steps related to human resources, such as steps 9 through 12.

It's easy to get started when you use the EP process. There are no big actions, no announcements, and no investment; just the desire to start on it next Monday.

If you review the twelve steps in the recommended EP process, you will see that many of them are actions that are built into the management system and, therefore, they are ongoing. That is clearly the case with respect to steps 2—develop a productivity culture; 3—make productivity part of every manager's job; 4—measure productivity; 7—empower employees; 8—utilize networking; and 10—restructure the operation. Thus the EP system results in a continuous improvement in work effectiveness.

Some of the other steps in the EP process concerning excellence in staffing, performance management, and reward for performance should be built into the excellence of human resources management work. Then these, too, will become an ongoing part of management. This system thus becomes a natural part of the management of the company. Increasing productivity is then a natural ongoing management activity.

2

Executive Commitment to Productivity Management

The first step in the EP process of productivity improvement is to get the required level of executive commitment to productivity improvement. This isn't necessarily the most important step in productivity work, but it's the first step in a series of actions.

In the EP process, the commitment required of executives is to the effectiveness of work and sound management practices, not to some set of programs, practices, or dogma. Executive commitment to effective work is not usually difficult to get and involves little, if any, cash cost.

Need for Executive Commitment

The traditional approach to productivity work starts by getting an executive commitment, and that is what is done in the EP approach. However, the commitment sought in the EP process of productivity management is only to the achievement of high levels of work excellence. Executives must be informed about something as fundamental as an organized productivity improvement effort. It wouldn't be possible to proceed without executives knowing about any significant productivity effort, and such an effort would not likely be successful without at least executive concurrence.

As noted earlier, the EP productivity approach does not require a deep executive commitment. However, it is essential in the EP process to have executive commitment in the sense of a conscious support of work effectiveness and management practices to improve work effectiveness. The commitment is to managing for higher work excellence.

The level of executive commitment required is at least a willingness to give the EP process a chance. Executives must be willing to support productivity management work enough to provide a realistic opportunity to evaluate the EP system, a chance to prove or to disprove that the system works.

As there is measurable success in productivity management, executive commitment will become stronger. Executives will commit themselves to actions that improve organizational results.

Pick an organization or location where there is likely to be success. Look for managers or units that have a high potential for improved productivity and operating managers who have a high level of interest in the work. Consider applying productivity management practices in the human resources department. Human resources professionals should have a high interest and know-how in the subject of productivity. If they are successful in improving productivity in their own department, this would be a success case. In addition, human resources professionals would then have more credibility for doing such work elsewhere in the company.

Work specifically to get an executive commitment to productivity improvement in the following four ways:

1. Executives must be reasonably well informed about productivity and have basic information about productivity in their own organization.
2. Executives must be effective in their own work, or they must be thought to be effective.
3. Executives themselves should be good at managing direct reports in a way that will achieve high work excellence.
4. Executives must formulate and implement a few basic policies that are needed to make productivity management work possible.

Each of these elements or areas of executive commitment is essential to success in productivity work. Each of these elements deserves your consideration and may require some affirmative actions.

An Informed Executive Group

Productivity is a business issue. Therefore, executive management should be well informed about productivity in the organization. Executives should think that productivity is an important enough business issue that they want to be well informed about productivity management matters.

A lot has been written and said about productivity, and a lot of it is incorrect, exaggerated, or misleading. If your organization is going to do serious productivity work, your top people must have correct information about productivity issues. That information must be true and practical and must relate to established enterprise goals. Otherwise, executive commitment to productivity may collapse with the first serious challenge or complaint about work to improve productivity.

Executives should have a good understanding of the relationship between performance, productivity, and business results. I have found this understanding to be critical in productivity management work. Most important, I think, informing executives about productivity involves calculating the impact of improved productivity on the company's operations. You should demonstrate how greater productivity might impact the achievement of the strategic goals of the company. Include information about the cost of productivity improvement efforts. Be as specific as possible about the practical "bottom-line" results that might likely accrue. Do this work as much as possible in the way important matters are usually communicated in the organization. Be brief, specific, and factual. Then the executives will decide.

An informed executive group will likely want to have a plan for productivity improvement and a strategy for doing the work. This information should be clear, direct, and honest.

If the EP process is to be used, a summary of the twelve action steps outlined in Chapter 1 should be communicated to the executives. Executives or the board may want information about what other others do with respect to productivity management. Be a reporter in this work, not an advocate. Make certain that the information you present is correct and responsive to executive interests. Use cases when they are relevant and do your reporting in a clear, businesslike manner. Provide information about likely problems or issues and risks of any type. Executives are entitled to all relevant information.

Only correctly and adequately informed executives will likely make a commitment to productivity improvement efforts and sustain that commitment over a period of time. Executives who are well informed will also be able to deal with issues or questions that will inevitably arise.

Some executives have used information about productivity to induce higher productivity in their own companies. For many years, for example, I saw that done with great skill at Collins and Aikman. All of my work for that company was in their New York office, where they had a very small staff. All they wanted me to do with respect to productivity was to keep the chief executive officer well informed. Don McCullough, the chief executive officer, would then take the information from those briefing sessions and use it when he was out in the organization. McCullough's theory was that if the operating managers knew he was interested in productivity and well informed, they would be far more attentive to the subject.

Productive Executives

In productivity consulting projects, this question is sometimes asked: On what group of employees should we focus our productivity efforts? I was first asked this question at Lincoln National Life, where the executives had already made a commitment to productivity improvement. My answer was that the focus should first be with the executives and managers because of the importance of their productivity and the way it was leveraged through the organization to affect the productivity of many others. This is often a politically incorrect view. The politically correct answer is to focus productivity improvement work on "them," with "them" meaning mostly hourly and office workers.

The fact is that executives must be productive, or at least perceived as such, if there is to be high productivity throughout the organization. Workers will probably be less inclined to increase their productivity if they think that executives are unproductive or don't care about their own personal effectiveness.

The productivity of executives and management people is, in fact, very important because the performance spread between acceptable and optimum effectiveness at these levels is so great. Furthermore, it is in these levels of jobs that there is the greatest number of discretionary items of work, and executives may do useful or useless work and do it either productively or unproductively.

As executives increase their own productivity, they become better informed about productivity in general. Then they are better able to help others in the organization increase *their* productivity. As executives increase their own productivity, they are also likely to become more convinced that it can be done—and probably have a deeper belief that increasing the effectiveness of work is worth doing. All of this contributes to greater productivity and a greater executive commitment to effective work.

If executives improve their own productivity, this certainly communicates to others in the organization that productivity is an important issue. When others observe executives being attentive to their own effectiveness, they will surely get the productivity message.

Productivity at the top sets an example. There is a ripple effect throughout the entire organization. The trickle-down theory really works in productivity management.

I can think of many top executives whose effectiveness had a ripple effect throughout their organizations. Their commitment to personal excellence contributed to greater effectiveness throughout their company. I won't use current executives as examples because to mention some would be to omit others. But we can see the powerful effect of executive commitment to personal work excellence by the documented history of some of the legends of business. Although I never personally met Messrs. Hall, Disney, or Penney, I worked for Hallmark, Disney, and

J. C. Penney shortly after each had left the business he founded. The respect for their competence had an overwhelming impact on the organizations for many years after they left. People would always use them as a standard. At Disney, for example, I would never know what to say when someone would ask, "What would Walt do about this?"

Effective Executive Productivity Managers

Executive commitment to productivity management should be reflected in part by how well those executives manage the productivity of their subordinates. Excellence in managing the effectiveness of the work of subordinates results in greater effectiveness and demonstrates a clear commitment to productivity. Productivity may then be leveraged from the top, as executives set good examples *and* to the extent that executives do a good job of productivity management for their direct reports. Then how well those direct reports manage the effectiveness of those who report to them leverages productivity even more. That's leveraging in productivity.

Leveraging productivity is an argument for applying productivity programs to executives and having them as active participants. However, executive time is limited, and the time cost of their involvement may be substantial. Executive support is more crucial to the success of productivity programs than the executive's participation in the program. Also recognize that executive productivity is different in important respects from the productivity of many. For example, doing the right thing is often more important for executive productivity than the efficiency of work.

I would also urge you to be careful about making the productivity efforts of the organization contingent upon executive involvement. Executives may just say no, and then there will be no productivity work.

It's important to note that productivity leveraging can start at any level in the organization. It's best to start leveraging productivity at the top, but this isn't essential. There have been cases where top executives were not good at managing the productivity of their subordinates. In some of these cases, the managers a few organizational levels lower were effective in managing productivity. In these cases, the top executives condoned and permitted the effective management of productivity work lower in the organization.

Policies

Essentially, there are three basic policy areas that are important in the EP process of productivity management. As part of a commitment to productivity, executives must set the following policies clearly and enforce each of them vigorously.

1. There must be a clear performance policy conveying the idea that higher performance on the part of every employee and every group of employees is a key objective of the firm.
2. There must be policies relating to the human cost of productivity improvement. These must essentially commit the company to paying the full cost of productivity improvement.
3. There must be policy guidelines relating to conflicts between the performance policy and what may be a conflicting interest in compliance.

Every manager must be aware of the company's policies in these three areas. If the policies don't exist, do what is possible to formulate and implement them at whatever level you manage.

There must be strong and specific policies relating to the improved performance of individuals and groups and in support of performance management. Ideally, the organization would have a policy requiring performance-based selection in both promotion from within and when people are brought in from the outside. A performance policy would also result in performance-based layoffs.

To support productivity management, there should be a strong performance pay policy. This must cover salary reward for performance, incentive bonus payment systems, and success-sharing plans.

There is often a human cost for productivity improvement. This may involve termination, downgrading, transfer, or diminished status. A company should pay the entire human cost of productivity improvement. That's the right thing to do. There is also reason to believe that if a company is to get an employee commitment to productivity, it must pay the human cost. Employees probably won't want to work to improve productivity if the result is that they are terminated or demoted.

The human cost of productivity for someone who is terminated means pay continuation and maintenance of benefits until the employee gets another job. That cost may involve training, outplacement, and relocation. Downgraded employees should not have their pay reduced. This is an example of the company paying the entire human cost of productivity improvement.

This issue has always proven to be a very difficult one. Companies will usually pay some of the human cost of productivity improvement for some employees. Many companies resist the idea of paying the entire cost, even though they paid such costs before the productivity improvement effort. It is my belief that paying the entire cost of productivity is a way for companies to gain employee commitment. The investment required may be substantial, but it is in direct proportion to improved operating effectiveness.

Clearly, there cannot be high productivity at the expense of safety. High productivity must also be accomplished within the limits of the law. So the policy must be the highest productivity within the law and with due regard for safety.

Policy matters relating to conflicts with compliance are simple in theory. You strive for high levels of productivity within the spirit as well as the letter of the law. Today, however, that simple policy is often challenged, and organizations are tempted to make exceptions to keep peace, maintain tranquility, and stay out of court.

I am not an attorney, but I think it's absolutely correct to say that a performance culture is totally compatible with the law. I also think that an employer has an obligation to tell employees if the law, or some application of the law, ever compels that employer to discriminate against higher performing employees.

An executive commitment to productivity policies represents

the first critical issue that will likely be faced in productivity management work. Therefore, written and enforceable personnel policies are needed. Among all companies, I would estimate the following:

- Clearly, less than half of all companies have an effective performance policy, and less than half of them pay properly for performance.
- About half of all companies do nothing about the human cost of productivity improvement except to apply their regular termination pay practices. Not one in a hundred companies pays the full cost of productivity improvement at this time.
- More than half of all companies discriminate against performance and have a bias against productivity in order to meet compliance goals.

These are not the policy conditions that are conducive to productivity improvement. These policy matters require urgent consideration.

Executive Involvement

Executive commitment and executive involvement are two distinctly different things. As discussed earlier, commitment relates to support for productivity improvement efforts, such as the EP process. Involvement relates to hands-on activities by a manager to support productivity activities throughout the organization and personal participation by the executive. For example, executives may be expected to attend productivity training sessions.

Opinion is divided about executive involvement in productivity work. For example, one of the large consulting firms doing TQM work argues that the chief executive officer must personally do eight things, which are typical of the views of those favoring a personal involvement in productivity by executives. Added to these eight points are my own comments.

1. *They say*: The chief executive officer must work with em-

ployees to determine what the company should be.

I say: Most employees wouldn't have any notion of what the company should be. Executives had better look to the customers and those who finance the business in determining what the company should be.

2. *They say*: Executives must emphasize customer service, not cost cutting.

   I say: Let's have everyone emphasize both.

3. *They say*: The chief executive officer must be willing to change everything.

   I say: If it ain't broke, don't fix it.

4. *They say*: The chief executive officer should personally set up pilot programs when employees think they know how to solve problems.

   I say: The chief executive officer should not be the training director or a project coordinator.

5. *They say*: Executives should pay employees when the company serves its customers better.

   I say: Reward everyone for improving performance.

6. *They say*: Executives must let employees participate and then let them implement what they suggest.

   I say: Productivity improvement is serious work, not playtime.

7. *They say*: Keep workers informed about all productivity programs by continuous communication and celebration of successes.

   I say: Productivity is serious work, not entertainment time.

8. *They say*: The chief executive officer must stay actively involved throughout the quality effort.

   I say: We need executive commitment as described earlier, not playacting.

These "they say" guidelines for senior executive involvement are rather typical of the views of TQM consultants. I think it is gross overinvolvement. In the EP process, no executive involvement is required except for the formulation and enforcement of basic policies that facilitate productivity improvement, personally productive executives, executives managing their direct reports for high levels of productivity, and executive leadership.

The Executive Coordinator

There is a special case of executive involvement that involves what is sometimes called the executive coordinator. The executive coordinator spends time in the organization carrying the productivity message, monitoring the work, making sure that productivity improvement work is being done, and evaluating managers of units and locations as to how well they are doing the productivity job. This executive coordinator can also be helpful in applying executive clout and commanding special resources when they are needed for productivity management. The executive coordinator clearly communicates executive commitment.

The value of an executive coordinator is potentially substantial and must be weighed against the problems of having an executive coordinator. The executive coordinator's job takes a lot of the time of some high-level person. That means the executive coordinator costs a lot of money. The job gets the executive coordinator involved in all types of detailed operational issues. There aren't that many executives who can be effective in a heavily operational curricula. The executive coordinator must have the ability to carry out the role without becoming a productivity czar.

I saw the executive coordinator role work at its best at McCormick during the late 1980s and early 1990s. McCormick's executive coordinator went to every location as a visible show of top management's commitment to higher productivity and to evaluate just how well the productivity job was being done. The first coordinator was the former vice president of human resources management, who had been promoted to the office of the chief executive officer. He was a personnel professional and well versed in productivity management. The success at McCormick, in my opinion, was not only that the role of the executive coordinator was correctly structured, but that they had the right person for the task.

Normally, the existing management organization has executive coordinators. The chief executive officer is the chief productivity coordinator. The heads of each business unit are executive coordinators for their business areas. Each operating manager is an executive coordinator. Only if the existing organization proves incapable of doing the productivity management job should a company consider using an executive coordinator.

Commitment to Excellence

Ideally, what you want is an executive commitment to *excellence*, not executive involvement in activities. The executive commitment to excellence should be endemic to the organization and reflective of everything the organization does. It isn't enough to be a "bottom-line manager," which mostly means concern only for this year's profits. Excellence means work of outstanding quality and superior merit. The results of the work must be better than that of others, namely, the competitors.

Ideally, a commitment to work excellence by executive management must be so clear and pervasive that a desire for excellence exists throughout the organization. In my mind, this is the essence of organizational leadership.

When there is a high executive commitment to productivity work as well as executive leadership, there will likely to be a commitment to excellence by everyone in the organization. With that kind of environment, there will likely be optimum performance by each person, optimum employee productivity for each organizational unit, and optimum business productivity for the enterprise overall. This is a strategy for business success that any organization can adopt: business success by work excellence. It is a strategy for any size company or for any unit in a company.

A commitment to excellence includes a commitment to hard work. That doesn't mean a sweatshop or even a stressful environment. But you will never find high levels of effectiveness by any person or group where there is not a commitment to hard work.

3

Develop an Effectiveness Ethic

The second step in the EP process is to achieve a high level of productivity consciousness on the part of everyone in the organization. The goal is to make every worker aware of the need for high levels of effectiveness and become highly committed to work excellence. Ideally, the goal is to get every person to be an effective manager of his or her own productivity and an activist in favor of greater productivity throughout the organization.

The objective is to have every person think productivity all the time. Have workers at every level of the organization continuously look for better ways of doing necessary work. Improving the excellence of work and increasing work effectiveness should become a natural condition of work.

In this step, you build an effectiveness ethic in each worker, or create more of an effectiveness ethic. Then, as many workers have more of an effectiveness ethic, the organization evolves a productivity culture.

The Effectiveness Ethic

The effectiveness ethic is a set of views, attitudes, and values that induces people to do their best at work. The effectiveness ethic is an inclination to do your best each and every time. When there is an effectiveness ethic, those attitudes are as automatic as breathing. They become so much a part of the consciousness of employees that doing one's best is the natural way and the only way.

This second step in the EP process is, in my view, crucial to success in increasing productivity. Experience has shown that it's possible to have a limited or conditional executive commitment to productivity but that there must be a high level of commitment to productivity by managers and workers at every level of the organization. The effectiveness ethic is essential to high productivity because workers increasingly possess essential knowledge and control the output of more machines, like computers.

Many publicized productivity programs recognize the importance of what I call the effectiveness ethic and productivity culture. For example, total quality management programs sometimes make massive efforts to get employee commitment to work excellence.

The effectiveness ethic is different from the work ethic. The work ethic involves an acceptance of the notion that everyone has to work and that work is part of life. With the work ethic, people are required to work effectively, often in a prescribed manner. To some extent, the work ethic reflects a belief in the moral benefits of work, and hard work is sometimes perceived as strengthening character.

The effectiveness ethic focuses on the rewards of work excellence and the need for good work rather than an obligation to work. This view values doing work the best way, not necessarily in some prescribed manner or in the traditional way.

When there is an effectiveness ethic, workers constantly seek a better way to accomplish required work. The effectiveness ethic requires a commitment to productivity for positive reasons, such as personal gain and self-esteem, whereas the work ethic emphasizes obligations and requirements. I think this distinction is important in productivity management work, partly because the effectiveness ethic is positive motivation and the work ethic is not. Positive motivation is always more enduring, more reliable, and stronger. However, positive motivation is also more difficult to implement.

The effectiveness ethic is also important because of the changes taking place at work. For example, as workers increas-

ingly control the machines, self-motivation is increasingly important to effective work. The effectiveness ethic is most relevant
when technology is possessed by the workers and when more
latitude is inherent in the work that is done. Then initiatives for
better work excellence are critical to productivity work in more
jobs, and productivity improvement initiatives are more likely as
there is more of an effectiveness ethic.

It is my opinion that we have been witnessing the evolution
of this effectiveness ethic for some time. This evolution has been
occurring mostly in smaller companies, in high-tech organizations, and in nonunion operations, which are the growing sectors
of the economy. The effectiveness ethic has been evolving among
working people partly because of knowledge about the consequences of low effectiveness of work as well as the changing
nature of work. Workers have learned about the need for effectiveness from their own experiences and from the experiences of
others.

There has been a tidal wave of information about jobs lost
because of low productivity and about the impact of international
competition. The media have caused working people to gain a
better understanding that high living standards are dependent
upon high levels of productivity.

You won't find many workers in this country today who have
not personally experienced losing a job or who have not had a
relative or friend who lost a job. Many workers who have lost
good paying jobs think that the loss of a good job to an overseas
worker was partly due to shoddy work, poor quality, and make-
work practices. These harsh lessons helped to spread the effectiveness ethic.

When there is an effectiveness ethic, people are inclined to
do their best. Then they have pride, and the power of pride can
be very great. With pride, there is higher self-esteem and that
creates confidence at work and higher job satisfaction. These
behavior characteristics provide a self-renewing momentum to
constantly strive for excellence of work.

More and more workers also know from experience that
doing unproductive work or working to poor quality standards
isn't satisfying. Poor work isn't necessarily easier to do than good
work.

As more employees fill jobs with a higher knowledge content and have more latitude of action, work results are based more on people's choice of work practices. When the method of work is at the control of the individual, the effectiveness ethic contributes to natural choices of more productive practices. Workers' natural inclination is to choose more effective methods of work, and as they do this, productivity will increase.

The effectiveness ethic is growing partly because informed workers, with a choice of being more effective, *are* being more effective. This is free choice at work. Free choice at the workstation and in organizational units is just as powerful as free choice in product markets.

Developing the effectiveness ethic in a formal manner to become a part of the productivity consciousness of the organization is an important step in the EP process. It turns every person in the company into a productivity manager and an advocate for higher productivity.

A Productivity Culture

The effectiveness ethic is a personal attribute. As more and more employees develop an effectiveness ethic, striving for excellence becomes a part of a company's culture. In the EP process, the focus is on building the effectiveness ethic into the consciousness of many or all employees, which causes an organizational culture to evolve.

There has been a lot of talk about company culture in the past ten years and most of it has been pretty theoretical. To me, company culture has always meant the styles and practices of conducting operations that have grown over time, that have become consciously understood throughout the organization, that significantly influence decisions and actions, and that will tend to be self-perpetuating unless they are altered.

What you seek over time is to have the effectiveness ethic so widespread in the workplace that the work culture is a productivity culture. Doing the best work possible and constantly striving for improvement become the standards for company work.

It is extremely important to recognize that the type of productivity culture desired is very different in various fields of work. In all cases, productivity is output per man-hour. But what constitutes output varies, based upon the essential characteristics of the work area and customer requirements. For example, before AT&T was broken up, the company's Western Electric organization made all of the telephones for the system. Productivity at Western Electric meant a telephone that always worked. The reliability of the telephone had to be almost 100 percent to serve customer requirements. In this country, people expect the telephone to work every time. Talking about this in a speech at Rancho Bernardo in California some years ago, the then chief executive officer of AT&T pointed out to its top managers that being 99 44/100 percent perfect was not nearly good enough for the telephone company, because that would mean millions of errors each year. Therefore, they needed zero defect output and that was essential to the productivity thinking at Western Electric.

In defense work, reliability has always been the essence of productivity. No one wants to be defended by a missile produced by a company that was awarded the contract because of high efficiency, low cost, and questionable reliability.

From the years that I worked at Raytheon, I know that reliability was number one in defense work. Everything done at our plants was to ensure the highest reliability of our missiles and electronics warfare products. Effectiveness was emphasized, but effectiveness meant reliability first and foremost.

During my consulting career I worked for a number of hospitals. At St. Luke's Hospital and the Catholic Charities hospitals in New York City, some of that work was on increasing employee productivity. The productivity of the clinical staff emphasized professional excellence, and productivity in most of the nonclinical operations largely meant caring.

At Black & Decker back in the 1960s, when Al Decker was still chief executive officer and the company was only in the power tool business, productivity was essentially a matter of highly efficient production. Engineering designed quality products, and manufacturing made them more efficiently than anyone else. In those days, even the Japanese could not compete with Black & Decker on price, even though Black & Decker paid its employees very well.

Working for Brown University, I learned that output in colleges meant learning and the nature or quality of the learning experience. This may be why so many productivity programs that are based on the quality of work life and better interpersonal relationships came out of the university environment.

Think carefully about what productivity means in your own operations and understand the key success elements of your operations. This is the key to focusing on what work excellence really means and the type of effectiveness you want to evolve.

Be very clear and practical about what it is you want to achieve. You need an effectiveness ethic that reflects your business essentials, *and* in those terms you are seeking to have a stronger productivity culture than your competitors.

There are no absolute standards for excellence. I urge companies to be more productive than their competitors and to improve so they are better than they were.

Action Steps

For whatever it's worth, over the many years that I worked in the area of productivity management, I found that it was always relatively easy to get an executive commitment. Executives will probably always commit to higher work effectiveness, which ultimately means better organizational results, at least on a conditional basis if the cost is modest.

By contrast, I always found it difficult to get a sufficient commitment to greater work effectiveness from managers and workers throughout the organization. Employees and managers can have many reasons why they lack enthusiasm for increasing productivity, or they may have concerns about productivity improvement actions. Some managers and employees have had bad experiences with productivity improvement efforts sometime in their work lives. Others may fear losing their jobs or having their status diminished. For some it is enough to lack enthusiasm for productivity improvement because the result may be more difficult work and painful changes.

There are a number of action steps that you might consider to build an effectiveness ethic. You should consider many views and experiences on this subject. Following are the action steps that I have found to be the most effective.

Communication

Communicate productivity at every opportunity. Preach productivity. Become an activist for work effectiveness. Become personally committed to improving productivity, and talk about productivity all the time. Each person who is dedicated to effective work can communicate productivity messages, regardless of the job he or she holds. An operating manager can speak with intelligence and authority about the value of work effectiveness in his or her own organization. Staff people, like human resources professionals or accountants, have many opportunities to talk about improving productivity throughout an organization.

When I was doing personnel project consulting, I had a dozen or so productivity messages. Each was five minutes or less. Some were one-liners, "sound bytes." If I did consulting work for your company in any area of personnel, you would have heard most of these productivity improvement messages. This illustrates one way of communicating productivity to gain an effectiveness ethic, and you might want to consider this approach.

Employees are a captive audience, an audience that receives communications about work all the time. Include productivity messages in your communications.

As work issues are considered, explore the impact of each on productivity. For example, many personnel issues, such as staffing and training, have work effectiveness implications. So every time things like staffing and training are discussed, be sure to explore very specifically the degree to which actions being considered will affect productivity. That's the right thing to do, and it is more effective communications on productivity that build an effectiveness ethic.

Talk about actual cases of productivity improvement. Sometimes you can illustrate how something similar might be done in your organization.

Talk about productivity like an evangelist. Be practical and truthful, but *sell* productivity. Truthfulness and relevance are important in communicating productivity messages. Some productivity experts tend to diminish the effectiveness commitment by talking in generalities and using cliches and platitudes.

Persistence is the key to building an effectiveness ethic by communication. Tell the productivity story again and again.

Set High Goals

If you seek an effectiveness ethic, you're more likely to get it if there is a commitment to something worthwhile. High but attainable goals thus contribute to an effectiveness ethic.

High goals can cause excitement. Exciting projects are worth talking about. That talk gets more communication about productivity and that will likely get more commitment to work effectiveness.

High but attainable goals are motivational. They tend to encourage people to stretch themselves. Stretching people can result in effectiveness levels never before thought to be possible. When people achieve higher levels of effectiveness, they become productivity believers and communicate the effectiveness ethic to others.

Set high but attainable goals in every way. Operating managers should do this in job assignments and in scheduling day-to-day work. If you use some type of objective-setting system, make sure these goals are high. Set high goals in budgets and in annual operating plans. Put high goals into the strategic goals of your company and make sure that one of those strategic goals is high but attainable productivity improvement.

In some cases, goal-setting has been considered as a separate productivity action step in productivity improvement work. This might logically be the case in companies that practice management by objectives. Whether it is an independent productivity action step or not, setting high goals contributes to the evolution of an effectiveness ethic.

Recognize Achievement

The recognition of high productivity achievement communicates effectiveness and honors productivity successes. Such recognition enhances the effectiveness ethic.

Some people think that productivity achievements should be "celebrated." I don't agree, but this is something for you to consider. Celebrations involve formal events with ceremony and festivities. That may create a carnivallike atmosphere, and these are work matters. Celebrations may cheapen work, and if the productivity accomplishment is small, then celebration trivializes the whole productivity effort.

If you think that celebration is important, start by celebrating accomplishments directly with the achievers. Make sure they realize that you know what was achieved and that their achievement is important and valued. But be careful not to give special recognition for accomplishing what is expected. If there is to be a celebration, save it for truly extraordinary accomplishments.

Remember that most productivity improvement comes from very ordinary achievements. In well-managed companies, a lot of the productivity achievement happens because many people are doing what they are supposed to do somewhat better, day by day and incident by incident.

Reward Productivity Improvement

Proper reward for greater productivity should include financial reward, which is covered in Chapter 13. The point here is simply that one way to get an effectiveness ethic and build a productivity culture is with proper reward systems.

Reward *is* recognition, and reward is a powerful method of communication. Pay rewards are essential, but there are also nonfinancial rewards. Reward productivity accomplishments with immediate and personal recognition. Sometimes saying "thank you" or "good work" is all that is needed.

Some people think that symbolic recognition awards, such as a letter from the president or a trinket bonus, help to create an effectiveness ethic. I think that such things are questionable, that they may be unproductive and detract from productivity, and that token recognition awards make productivity work seem as unimportant as the token award.

Success

Perhaps the best way of getting an effectiveness ethic throughout the organization is by success in increasing productivity. If there are enough productivity successes, the executives will likely become more committed to productivity management. Successes in productivity work can cause more of an effectiveness ethic.

Productivity successes are easy to communicate and can be made interesting. Productivity successes make high goals seem more attainable and more worthwhile pursuing.

Success is what should be recognized, not symptoms of success or achieving things that are not provably related to work excellence. And for those involved, success is, of course, in part its own reward. Thus success supports the achievement of an effectiveness ethic in a number of ways.

Operational Leadership

Operating managers at every level of the organization are the ones who must help workers become more effective. It is the operating managers who must be the ones to get employees to strive for excellence. Where there is a striving for excellence, there will be an effectiveness ethic.

I have seen many leadership studies in my thirty-three years of consulting. In one way or another, all of them showed that those considered leaders at the operating management level always possessed the following two characteristics:

1. They managed successful operations, and at least part of the success was because of higher organization productivity.
2. Workers think the managers made them better and more effective, and encouraged them to strive for excellence.

Effective managers who exhibit productivity leadership also tend to help their people do better in productivity management activities. People like to do what they do well. If they do a good job of productivity improvement work, they will be inclined to do more of that work.

Commentary

Achieving a high effectiveness ethic is one of the four critical and required action steps in productivity management. It is also one of the most difficult to accomplish. Developing an effectiveness ethic is thus worth deep thought. It is often the pivotal issue in productivity management work. Following are some additional thoughts and some commentary about building an effectiveness ethic.

High work effectiveness and an effectiveness ethic also depend on values. The values don't relate to niceness, good interpersonal relationships, getting along, or being a team player. These values relate to striving for excellence. Doing one's best is the high moral ground at work.

Not everyone agrees with this view. Most who have worked on productivity do agree that some values have some impact on an effectiveness attitude. Therefore, this difficult issue of values is part of work on the effectiveness ethic.

There are those who think that the action steps I have identified are insufficient. Some of these people favor a massive and continuing effort at building an effectiveness ethic. The old quality circles system paid an enormous amount of attention to effectiveness attitudes as do some (but not all) of the variations of total quality management. You will find a lot of literature and some cases that urge massive attention to getting a productivity culture. For example, Philip Crosby's "quality is free" view grew out of his experiences with quality control at ITT. Hal Geneen's management style at ITT was always spending massive management attention on each major problem, and that approach was also applied to quality problems at ITT. In some companies where these massive efforts to build an effectiveness ethic have been applied, there were strong unions that opposed productivity improvement. In other cases, there had been bitter experiences in the past with productivity improvement work. In these special cases, it may be necessary to launch massive efforts to build an effectiveness ethic. In most cases by far, however, the six action steps described plus an executive commitment to productivity improvement will be more than sufficient to evolve a productivity culture.

Recognize that there has been a lot of bad experience with productivity improvement in the past. In fact, in many organizations, productivity is a dirty word, and companies will go to great lengths to avoid using the word because of past experiences.

However, changing words cannot change history. Productivity management called anything else is still productivity management. The really critical thing is to be sure that your current efforts don't turn out to be bad experiences. Then whatever you call your productivity program now will also become a dirty word.

There are plenty of reasons to think that the massive efforts to create an effectiveness ethic are the productivity mistake of the 1990s. In too many cases, these massive efforts have turned into cults, not just fads. The theatrics, TQM speak, and playacting that go with massive efforts for an effectiveness ethic often seem ingenuous and almost childlike to employees. In your situation it may be necessary to do more than the six recommended action steps to gain more of an effectiveness ethic, or to do some of those actions in extreme ways. But recognize that there is a high cost and substantial risk of failure when you undertake massive efforts to get people to embrace an effectiveness ethic. The very reasons that cause you to take extraordinary actions may be the reasons why you fail anyway.

The economics of productivity is such that even small gains can pay for a lot of effort to gain more of an effectiveness ethic. This is what has driven some to do such extraordinary and occasionally bizarre things to gain more of an effectiveness ethic. In an organization of 1,000 workers, a 1 percent productivity increase might justify the cost of a half-dozen full-time persons selling the effectiveness ethic among the other 1,000 employees. That is illustrative of exactly what some well-known companies have done with their total quality management programs.

You could argue that if everyone in the company was committed to high levels of work excellence, the organization has an effective productivity effort. Talented people who have an effectiveness ethic will be productive. That *is* productivity management in an ideal organization. I have never seen such an organization, and I don't think one exists. The chances are that no matter how good an organization may be, it can always improve by having more of an effectiveness ethic. Increasing the effectiveness ethic will almost always result in higher productivity.

The absence or presence of an effectiveness ethic has an effect on other action steps in productivity management work. A high effectiveness ethic supports all the action steps recommended here and those described in the next ten chapters.

There are many effective organizations and many where work effectiveness is terrible, regardless of how productivity is defined in that operation. However it happened, in every case of high productivity I know, there is also a strong effectiveness ethic. And in every case I know where productivity is very low, there is a low effectiveness ethic. That is convincing proof that an effectiveness ethic and high productivity go hand in hand, and it seems reasonable that the effectiveness ethic is a cause of higher productivity rather than a result of higher productivity.

Productivity work can be postponed and that may detract from urgency about an effectiveness ethic. In good years, managers sometimes say they don't need an improvement in productivity, and in bad years those same managers may say the company can't afford it. Intangible activities like building an effectiveness ethic in particular can be postponed. In fact, when productivity improvement projects are undertaken, there is often an urge to skip this step and go on to more tangible activities, such as downsizing.

Where there are unionized employees, there will be more difficulties in building an effectiveness ethic. The greatest failure of the unions in this country may well be their reluctance to support productivity improvement. Unions have a commitment to improving the working conditions of their members and to preserving their union status. This generally means that they will accept or condone productivity improvement only if the alternative is clearly loss of jobs or diminished status for their members or decertification. That's why unions in smokestack industries have reluctantly and half-heartedly gone along with some productivity improvement efforts. But unions of teachers and municipal employees have no fear of losing jobs to overseas competition so they have a low interest in productivity improvement.

Special interest groups have goals that also may be in conflict with an effectiveness ethic. In fact, most special interest groups seek special and preferential treatment for their constituents, and that is often in conflict with an effectiveness ethic.

Productivity progress from productivity programs tends to be a one-time event with a finite life cycle. Productivity actions initiated by workers with an effectiveness ethic are continuous and self-renewing and become a way of working.

Evolving an effectiveness ethic involves basic building activities, the infrastructure of productivity management. It tends to be unglamorous but essential work. Understanding this leads to the conclusion that the job in this step of the EP productivity process is to start an effectiveness ethic, not to achieve the desired level of an effectiveness ethic before proceeding with other action steps. Building effectiveness attitudes and a productivity culture is an ongoing activity and a continuous management job.

In evolving an effectiveness ethic, focus on the managers first. Urge managers to work on evolving an effectiveness ethic with other workers.

When you examine methods and action steps to build an effectiveness ethic, it will be clear that it is mostly the direct managers of people who must accomplish this vital step. It is the managers who do the important communicating about productivity. It is the managers who set high goals. It is the managers who give recognition. Thus the managers are key to evolving an effectiveness ethic.

4

Organization for Productivity Management

The third step in the EP process of productivity management involves organization. It is recommended that the management organization that exists (or should exist) should be used for productivity management. There should never be a separate organization for productivity management.

The most important lesson I ever learned about productivity management occurred in 1976, shortly after my first book on productivity was published. Because of that book, I had been asked to speak to a management group from International Multifoods Company, which met at the John's Island Club in Vero Beach. This was my very first formal presentation on productivity. I presented my material and thought it went very well.

When I finished, the chief operating officer stood up and let me have it. He was nice enough but very clear. His message was that productivity was a management job and that he and his colleagues were doing their job of managing productivity the best they could. He said they had done the productivity management job for many years and didn't need a consultant like me to tell them to do their job!

He was right, of course, and I have been grateful to him ever since. Productivity *is* a management job. Productivity management has been done by managers since the beginning of time. My job and the task of all consultants, personnel professionals, and productivity gurus is to help those managers manage productivity better.

It is presumptuous for experts, many of whom have never managed, to think they know how to get higher worker excellence. It is a terrible mistake to give authority for productivity improvement work to anyone other than the operating managers.

The EP process fixes accountability for productivity management solely with every true manager. I think this is a critical issue and one where the EP process differs from some other productivity approaches you might consider.

A Manager's Job

In the EP process, productivity is part of every manager's job. Every manager of people is a productivity manager. When you communicate work matters to the managers, they must be told that part of their job is the effectiveness of work. If your company wrote job descriptions for managers, there would be statements about responsibilities for the effectiveness of the work of subordinates. Written or verbal, in job descriptions or however, managers must be told that productivity is a part of their job.

Whenever I want an example of making productivity an operating manager's job, I think of my experiences at the Jim Walter Corporation. Not surprisingly, this entrepreneurial-driven company expected every manager to be a Renaissance man, and high levels of effectiveness in productivity management were expected from every level of management. Jim Walter personally believed that, with higher level managers to guide them and some staff support, every manager should be able to do what Jim himself did in the early days of the business he founded after World War II.

And why not? Why can't a manager who has staff support and higher level management guidance do things like manage productivity?

The authority to manage people is never complete and without limitation. There are limitations because of laws that limit authority. For example, a manager has enough authority to be said to manage productivity if that manager must make management decisions without consideration of race or sex. In addition, a manager is not crimped in the ability to get effective results by lawful behavior toward others at work. Even if laws require unproductive practices, managers must get the most effective work possible within the legal requirements that exist.

There are also "company" laws. These are policies and requirements that must be followed, for whatever reason. For example, the next higher level of manager may, in practice, "review" personnel decisions in such detail that many decisions are made at the higher level. Laws and company requirements are the rules that managers must work within as they strive for high work effectiveness.

Assigning the productivity job to operating managers involves important issues. Who is responsible for work methods: the industrial engineer or the operating manager? Who is responsible for employment selections: the personnel organization or the manager? Unless the answer to all such questions is essentially "the operating manager," then the manager can't be perceived as having been assigned the productivity job.

Support people and professionals should help and advise but not manage. For example, industrial engineers apply their professional knowledge to determine methods of work, but it should be the operating manager who then accepts, modifies, or rejects these methods. The same thinking applies to personnel issues.

I urge that every operating manager in every company be granted authority that is equivalent to his or her counterpart in an independent company. Of course, with that authority goes accountability for prudent judgment and good results, including high levels of work excellence. Similarly, the recommendation to every manager is that he or she assumes the productivity management job to the maximum extent permitted by the company's management style. Push this to the limit of prudence.

Following are six important guidelines that must be considered in assigning the productivity management job to the operating managers.

1. It is necessary to structure the organization so there are real management jobs.

2. Organizational unit management is an important development in organizational structuring, and it should be considered in productivity management work.
3. The managing job must be delegated to the managers and only to the managers of people.
4. The managers themselves must be managed well.
5. Duplicate organizations set up for productivity improvement should be avoided at all costs.
6. Staff groups, such as personnel and all consultants, must perform only a support role in productivity management.

I think these are the important guidelines for effective management. Each is addressed in relation to productivity management in the following sections.

Organizational Structure

Organizational structure has importance largely because of its impact on the management of people. Thus organizational structure is an important management issue and has a direct relevance to assigning the productivity job to managers. In fact, some companies need a substantial restructuring of their organizations in order to improve management and productivity. Organizational restructuring is something for most companies to consider. When restructuring is done by making the organization flatter, one result is to increase the span of management (see Chapter 11).

A major organizational issue is the span of management, the number of people managed by a manager of personnel. On the average, the span of management today is a little more than five, which isn't sufficient for effective managing.

To carry out the responsibilities of a manager of personnel requires a considerable amount of personnel know-how and a substantial knowledge about a particular company's personnel practices. To acquire such knowledge requires considerable learning. Sustaining a satisfactory level of knowledge about personnel in order to carry out the responsibilities of the job of manager of personnel also requires time. It simply does not make economic sense to expect such a time investment if it is to be utilized for making decisions about only a few employees.

To make decisions about selection, training, pay, communications, and the like also requires *skill*. For example, you cannot really be good at interviewing if you do it only a few times a year. Effectively managing people involves excellence in the application of personnel knowledge, which requires practice and experience. This necessarily means managing a significant number of people.

Finally, the effective management of personnel is dependent upon experience and the precedents that many experiences can provide. You need to have a lot of experiences to develop the mature judgment of a good manager of personnel. You will likely have sufficient experience only if you manage a sufficient number of subordinates.

Thus there is an appropriate "span of management" of personnel that is necessary in order to acquire the knowledge of personnel required to do effective work and accumulate and sustain the required amount of skill and experience to manage people effectively. There are no scientific formulas for what this "span of management" might be, but, as a guideline, at least ten people should be supervised.

In high-level jobs with a great diversity of know-how and high technology, there probably can't be a span of management much more than ten. When diversity, technology, and levels of jobs are moderate, there should probably be between twenty and thirty direct reports. In some circumstances, the span of management may be fifty.

In the early 1990s, business started moving toward a greater span of management. There were two driving reasons: to get higher productivity and to reduce costs.

The principal method of increasing the span of management was simply to eliminate at least one organizational level. This required regrouping existing organizations, and that automatically increased the span of management. A survey conducted in 1991 showed that four of five companies either had streamlined their organizations by eliminating organizational levels in the last couple of years or were planning to do so in the next couple of years.

Increasing the span of management benefits productivity

management in a number of ways. The broader span makes it possible to focus more on managing and build skills and know-how in productivity management. Having more time and more manageable portions of time will also likely result in the acquisition of special productivity skills. For example, whereas a manager rarely knows more than his or her subordinates about the technology of their work or has better operations skills in a work area, the effective manager of people should often be the leading expert on *work processes*. There is a special know-how about how to proceed in different activities. This expertise can help all workers in the unit be more productive.

Spending more time on managing will likely result in the acquisition of skills needed to implement some of the important action steps in the EP process. I find this is particularly important in utilizing technology, removing unproductive practices, restructuring, networking, and manpower management.

Organizational Unit Management

A special opportunity for effective productivity management is the evolution of the organizational unit style. Organizational unit management is important to productivity management and is a basic management trend you should know about.

Organizational unit management isn't a totally new style of managing because companies have been organizing by business areas, divisions, and locations for a very long time. However, the organizational unit management approach establishes units much lower in the organization.

I first saw organizational unit management in action back in 1963, on a day many Americans remember—the day President Kennedy was shot in Dallas. I spent that day in meetings with the heads of businesses at Johnson & Johnson. It doesn't matter what the assignment was, but it was a big job and required a deep understanding of their organizational structure. I found that J&J had businesses within businesses within businesses, in some areas up to six levels of whole businesses. Later, a J&J executive told me that he was the chief executive officer of a company at age twenty-seven. The company was J&J in the Philippines, and there were only about two dozen employees. But it was a separate business and a separate organizational unit, and he was the general manager.

I always felt that a large part of J&J's vitality came from the culture of many layers of organizational units. J&J people say that this philosophy came from "the General" (Johnson), who set out to simulate the organizational dynamics he found in the army, right down to the platoon level.

The General was ahead of his time. It was not until the late 1980s that organizational unit management began to develop as an important business trend. I first reported this trend in *The Sibson Report* in 1990. It has evolved and been reported a number of times since.* I think it is a fundamental development in the art of management and is very important in the EP approach to productivity management.

What's happening is that more and more companies are establishing more and more operating units, and they are establishing them deeper in the organization. Sometimes this means profit and loss centers within profit and loss centers. Organizational units are often established below profit and loss centers, with partial profit and loss measures or statistical measures of unit performance.

The establishment of units with statistical measures of unit performance is not new. For example, there have been cost measures for factories. What is new is the number of statistical unit performance measures and the excellence of these measures.

There are usually a number of performance measures when profit and loss accounting measures can't be applied. One of these measures will almost always be *productivity*. All of this work is being facilitated by computers, which make it much more practical to record and report data that measure unit performance.

Organizational unit management supports and facilitates productivity management. For example, all organizational units are headed by real managers, and it is natural to assign productivity management to such managers. The units also provide more and better productivity measures.

*See *Strategic Planning for Human Resources Management*, pp. 201–203, AMACOM, New York, 1992.

It is difficult to describe the power and vitality of organizational unit management, but it simulates entrepreneurship. This tends to make the operating manager committed to effectiveness and more like an owner-manager than an administrator.

Organizational unit management combines the vitality, flexibility, and innovativeness of a small organization with the know-how and resources of a large one. That's why I think it is highly desirable and that's why it is a potentially important part of the EP process of productivity management.

Delegative Management

Assigning the productivity management job to managers means delegating authority to them. Delegative management was a key part of my book on employee productivity in 1976, and I believe that granting authority to managers to do the productivity management job is even more crucial now.

Delegative management is a style that grants the authority to act. Delegation is more than participation or involvement. It is authority. It's not a matter of listening, accepting suggestions, or going along with ideas. Delegation is letting the managers do it.

Managers delegate to subordinate managers the authority to make decisions, mostly about work methods. Those managers then empower employees to make work decisions. Delegation is to the managers of people; employees are empowered by their immediate manager.

In order to have delegative management, it is necessary to set policies, establish objectives, articulate the criteria for measuring performance, and set the standards of performance expected. With these guidelines, delegative management not only permits individual managers to determine the best way to do needed work, but it expects the managers who are accountable for the work to continuously devise special methods and procedures that will improve work effectiveness.

Delegative management works to push decision making down in the organization where it can be done at the lowest level and where the details of the operation are best known. It expects managers to innovate and continuously find better ways to operate. This includes better ways to increase the effectiveness of work done by subordinates.

When there is delegative management, every manager becomes directly accountable for work effectiveness; each is a productivity manager. Then there are many experienced and intelligent managers who know their own operation the best and who work to increase its effectiveness. This is a sure method of increasing productivity.

I don't know who invented delegative management, but I first learned about it when I started doing consulting work for Colt Industries. George Strichman had set up the company as twenty-seven separate businesses, each with a real president. These presidents were encouraged to delegate equivalently to subordinate managers in divisions, units, and locations.

There was real independence among those managers. When I went into the field, I was working for Crucible Steel or Chandler Evans or whatever business I was visiting, not the corporate office. Although I was paid by the corporation, I was there to help the business. These businesses were very independent but closely monitored. Strichman was the master of "loose-tight" management tactics.

Every one of the twenty-seven Colt businesses could be a case study in productivity management. The management job at Colt was to serve the customer and produce effectively. In the businesses that existed, producing effectively meant higher productivity. Each of the heads of those businesses knew that productivity management was a key part of their jobs.

Delegative management contributes to greater productivity mostly because the direct manager knows the work the best, knows the people, and understands the circumstances pertaining to the work. If you look at the recommended productivity action steps in this book, in some cases the managers are the only ones who can implement many of these steps, and they can implement them the best in most of the other cases.

Management of Managers

Delegative management cannot mean abdication of responsibility by higher level management. There is no reason for delegation to result in chaos. You can't have delegation without control. There can't be "lose" without appropriate "tight" monitoring and controls. In fact, the more authority is delegated, the more expert must be the management monitoring and control practices.

Companies have tried many methods of controlling management actions when there is delegative management. These have mostly involved rules for uniform behavior, close monitoring, review of actions, and delegating authority only on some matters. I think that the key to delegating authority prudently is a high skill in managing the managers. Managing the managers is a unique activity and involves very special skills and talents.

There hasn't been nearly enough focus on managing the managers, partly because it was not thought to be of importance until delegative management started to be adopted. The management of the managers who have great authority delegated to them is a critical matter in controlling and monitoring in a delegative management work style.

The managers of managers must themselves be experienced and skilled in managing. They must have great talent in understanding organizational unit performance measures. The managers of managers must be good coaches and skilled in mentoring. The managers of managers must have the authority to control and correct the managers.

Under delegative management, the success of an organizational unit is judged mostly by statistical performance measures and the excellence of the performance of those who work in the group. My view is that success is largely dependent upon the skill of higher level managers in managing the managers as well as the correctness of the methods of delegation in the first place and the talent of the managers who are granted authority.

A Separate Productivity Organization

The EP process emphasizes assigning the operating managers of personnel throughout the company the accountability for productivity management. The EP process contemplates authority for productivity management resting *only* with operating managers, although not without limit or restraint. The EP process assumes that the responsibility for productivity management is not shared with anyone else.

Sometimes it may be necessary to assign the productivity job, or a part of productivity management, to others for at least some time. I think this is always a mistake, but in some cases it is a matter you should consider.

When there is productivity bargaining, some of the work done by the managers may be assigned to a special project group. The bargaining is done by someone other than the managers. The argument for a special organization for productivity bargaining is that bargaining isn't management and that productivity bargaining may resemble a war rather than an operation.

A number of the well-known productivity programs have had separate organizations. The programs that did this include organizational development, quality circles, and total quality management. The reasons for these separate organizations were mostly that managers lacked the special know-how that was required, they did not have an appropriate attitude, or they lacked a sufficient commitment to the program itself.

I have always thought that separate organizations were unnecessary, except in very special circumstances such as contentious productivity bargaining. Furthermore, in most cases I know, the establishment of a separate organization did not work well and was abandoned before very long.

If you do consider extra organizations, think about the following points:

- Existing organizational units can do everything that a separate organization can do. If managers lack know-how, train them, or find managers who can do the entire management job now.
- The extra organization adds many hours of work, and this lowers productivity.
- Extra organizations may create more conflict and divisiveness in an organization. Simplicity and harmony are the allies of productivity.
- The backgrounds and experiences of these separate productivity persons are important. Often they have mostly

been qualified in some process that is neither management nor personnel.

* If separate organizations are of value for special, temporary purposes, then make sure they are temporary by setting a date for their termination.
* Extra organizations exist to take authority from operating managers, and that demeans and undermines operating management. This can cause long-term problems and weaken management overall. The effect of any separate organization on management is, I think, a major issue.
* In fact, extra organizations are often created to compel people to do things they would not otherwise do or to behave in a different way. But if these "things" and a certain "behavior" are good for the organization, why wouldn't the existing organization do these anyway?

The Role of the Human Resources Management Department

Consistent with the philosophy of assigning the productivity job to the operating managers, the staff organizations have only information and support roles under the EP approach. This guideline applies to all support jobs, but I use personnel as a case partly because productivity is about people and partly because personnel is the support work I know the best.

The EP process could operate without personnel experts. That's actually what happens in small, independent companies, and many small companies are very productive. So personnel staff support may be helpful in productivity management, but it is not essential.

Human resources management professionals may provide a lot of useful information and helpful support. The human resources professional could be a knowledge expert in the field of productivity management and a central information source for all operating managers to access. As knowledge experts, the human resources management department might be involved in a variety of projects and tasks relating to productivity. The human resources staff might work as internal consultants on productivity management. Under the EP approach, the human resources management department can also have an important monitoring role. For example, they might work to ensure true empowerment of employees.

Some of the recommended steps in the EP process are highly dependent upon effective human resources management department operations. This would include staffing, reward for performance, and manpower management. These areas provide an opportunity for substantial help and support by personnel professionals. In the EP process, however, human resources management professionals don't do any direct productivity management work, except managing the productivity of the human resources department. They may help if asked, but in the EP approach, operating managers are assigned the entire job of productivity management.

Consultants shouldn't do anything more than the company's human resources management staff under the EP process of productivity management. This may be another reason for the lack of enthusiasm for the EP approach by many large consulting firms.

Productivity Management Is a Manager's Job

Remember, the basic view of the recommended EP process is that productivity involves managing. Productivity management must be assigned to the operating managers. It is this step that dramatically distinguishes this particular process from other widely used methods. Most of the alternative methods of productivity management involve other people or groups having direct authority in at least some important areas related to productivity management.

There is a lot of flexibility in the EP process, but not on the critical issue of who manages productivity. When it comes to assigning authority for the management of productivity, there can be no sharing of authority. Within constraints, productivity is the accountability of operating managers.

Don't compromise on this issue. When I was doing project consulting, I would gracefully withdraw from a consulting assignment if there was any compromise on this vital point.

Management must manage. Management must manage the effectiveness of work. It's as plain as that.

There is often genuine concern about whether operating managers can do the productivity management job. They will be able to do it if they have any ability to manage and if there is an adequate span of management.

Under this EP method, all levels of managers, in every area and location, are assigned the job of managing productivity. This is a big issue in some companies. It is a reason why some reject the EP method. Even when EP has been adopted, I always found some key people who disagreed with this view.

Some managers and staff persons still cling to the centralized and bureaucratic management style. But under the EP process, they must change, and operating managers must be granted the authority to manage productivity. True, there is often genuine concern about the ability of managers to take on the productivity job. Whenever this concern proved to be correct, it was always about the first levels of managers, and it turned out they weren't really managers at all. First levels of managers are often schedulers, administrators, and assistants to the real managers.

There are also some very bright persons, mostly in academia and consulting firms, who really believe that they know how to manage better than bright and experienced managers. Some productivity experts really believe that they have discovered a brilliant method, never before conceived, that will be the magic way of achieving higher productivity. To my knowledge, all such brilliant methods fail.

At least consider using the organization you have before you add extra organizations. Give the managers the job of productivity, but also measure productivity results and evaluate managers' performance in part by how well they manage productivity.

5

Measuring Productivity

The fourth step in this recommended process is to measure productivity. Have performance measures for every person. Have productivity measures for every organizational unit. Have employee productivity measures for every P&L center and every business area. Have productivity measures for the company overall. Whenever possible, use multiple measures of productivity for each organizational unit. Have as many measures of productivity as practical. Make comparisons between organizational units internally. Make productivity comparisons with other companies. Develop productivity measurement standards.

You Must Measure Productivity

In this recommended method of productivity management, measuring productivity is critical. The EP process of productivity management is very measurement-oriented.

As already discussed, the basic strategy is to assign the productivity management job to managers. Then you must measure how well managers do that job with productivity data. All subsequent action steps are things managers might do, and the effectiveness of such actions would be measured by productivity data.

In the EP process, the measurement of productivity is a *required* activity, but it's not a heavy burden. Measuring productivity is essential for four reasons:

1. Productivity data are one important measure of operating results.
2. Such data are often diagnostic. Productivity data may provide early identification of problems and issues. Such data may help to analyze work situations and might indicate more productive ways to work.
3. The development of productivity measures requires thinking about work effectiveness, and such thinking may contribute to improved management.
4. Such data also indicate whether actions taken to improve productivity have been effective.

Following are comments about each of these reasons for productivity measures. You are urged to think more deeply about these in relation to your own organization.

Measuring Results

Productivity measures can be an important part of a reporting system of an organization. Productivity data complement financial income statements and balance-sheet reporting in the measurement of operating results.

Financial reporting is the only required results data and is the only information that must be reported to outsiders, including the government. Management needs more in-depth and sophisticated measures of results. So management uses various data to supplement required financial reporting, and productivity data can be one important part of that information reporting.

Productivity can be used to measures results for any type of operation. Therefore, these data are usable in any organization that can't apply P&L accounting information. This includes government operations and nonprofit operations of all types.

You can't really know the value of productivity in management until you use it to measure results. Such information not only helps to measure organizational effectiveness but also contributes to the development of a performance culture in an organization.

Diagnostic Measures

Whenever an individual performance measure declines, there should be concern. That is an indication of a problem, an early warning of what could be a severe problem. Productivity data can be a part of a company's reporting information for all levels of managers. Any level can then identify declines in productivity and consider appropriate actions.

Downtrends in productivity can be an early warning of trouble for any level of manager. The appropriate response may be an inquiry, which may be sufficient, or more aggressive corrective actions may be required.

Increases in productivity may provide useful information. Any unplanned and unexpected increase in productivity may be indicative of something the manager should be aware of. What caused the productivity increase might be used elsewhere in that manager's operation. Whatever caused the productivity increase might be of value in some other part of the company.

Keep in mind the relationship between performance, productivity, and organizational results. Productivity declines are a signal of likely future declines in profits, but they usually precede profit drops enough to make corrective actions possible.

Using productivity as a diagnostic tool and as early warning information is a classic case of proactive management. With timely identification of an emerging issue, productivity trends may make it possible to deal with the problem quickly and avoid a larger one later. In many cases, productivity data can be useful in analyzing a work situation or by providing information about the best work method. Many work models would use productivity data.

Work Intelligence

The process of developing productivity data measures often requires some deep thinking about the work being done. That often contributes to a greater understanding of the operation and a higher level of work intelligence. As productivity data is used, it may suggest a different view or emphasis on what productivity really is. Remember that productivity has a very different meaning and emphasis in different activities. Developing and using productivity measures enhance an understanding of the special meaning of productivity in an operation.

The quest for new measures of productivity should be never-ending, largely because one's understanding of productivity is rarely perfect. As intelligence about operations and conditions of work improves, more and better productivity measures may be possible.

Measuring Productivity Actions

An organization will never know whether some action to improve productivity really works unless there are productivity data measures. Why would organizations undertake the time and expense of a substantial productivity improvement effort unless they could measure the success of actions taken to improve productivity?

Too often, success in productivity management work is reported in generalities or anecdotes. Business literature is filled with claims of productivity success based on such phrases as:

"... resulted in better team attitudes"
"... was very successful"
"... had profound consequences"
"... resulted in better customer relations"

You could fill a 100,000-word book with these cliches. In the EP process, there must be productivity measures that are reported as hard data. In a survey of productivity practices, conducted in part to get information for this book, about one-third of the participating companies do not measure productivity in any area of their organization. Some of those who don't measure productivity said that their company does have an organized productivity program of some sort. I argue that you can't manage productivity unless you measure it.

Productivity Measures

There are many methods of measuring productivity. Each organization needs to develop its own measures. In large companies, there will likely be different types of measures for different units.

There are no standard measurement systems in productivity, nothing equivalent to the standard accounting practices used in financial reporting. There are no government regulations requiring the reporting of productivity data. However, there are many experiences and cases, and there is a variety of information that will help any organization develop productivity data.

First, believe that your organization can develop useful productivity measures for every organizational unit. Every organization that has set out to develop usable productivity data has been successful.

Following are five basic approaches to measuring productivity, and they can all be calculated and reported in hard data.

- Physical volume
- Dollarized productivity
- Ratio measures
- Value added
- Proxy measures

Physical Volume

The first productivity measures that were used were very direct and very simple. They were measures of physical volume divided by man-hours of work. Thus the basic model of employee productivity measure was simply:

$$\frac{\text{number of units produced}}{\text{man-hours of work}}$$

In many companies that use a measured day work system, physical output can be counted at each workstation. Then productivity measures are possible at each workstation and in each section of the operation by using the basic productivity formula.

When there are different kinds of products or services, physical volume measurements of productivity are more complex. The more the variation of what is done, the greater the complexity of developing and using physical productivity measures.

It is sometimes possible to develop productivity index measures. These are composites of production of different products. For example, in an organization that produced three basic products, which in combination represented 90 percent of the total physical output, the productivity index was:

$$P = \frac{.42 \text{ A products } + .37 \text{ B products } + .21 \text{ C products}}{\text{man-hours}}$$

The percentage applied to each product is based on the output of each product and the industrial engineering standards of the time required to produce each product. Composite indexes work only when there are a few products and when the products change infrequently.

Dollarized Productivity

A measure of effectiveness that has broad application is dollarized productivity. Dollarized productivity is simply dollar measures of output divided by payroll. A simple formula is:

$$P = \frac{\text{total sales}}{\text{total payroll}}$$

There are many variations of dollarized productivity data, and they can be used in any organization that has revenue data and assigned workers. Dollarized productivity data can be tracked over any period of time. Dollarized productivity is often used to determine trends and may also be used in intercompany productivity comparisons. Dollarized productivity measures are contaminated by such things as price changes and capital substitution. Statistical adjustments can be made for such items, but dollarized productivity measures are never precise.

Ratio Measures

Ratios of various types can be used as productivity measures. In personnel work, for example, personnel ratios are the ratio of personnel people to total employment. Sometimes the primary purpose of such ratios is manpower control, but they also provide a productivity measure.

Ratio measures are also used to measure the effectiveness of staff and support positions. Assuming equal or better services, declining ratios indicate higher productivity of staff and support work.

Ratios can be used as quality measures. The ratio of rework to original production work is an example.

All of these ratio measures are indirect and are only indications of the effectiveness of work. They are most useful as supplements to other productivity measures.

Value Added

Some companies develop quite analytic methods of value-added productivity measures. Value-added measures of productivity are by far the most difficult and complex.

Value-added productivity data measure the total dollar value of goods produced or services rendered, less the total dollar cost of all materials purchased. The difference represents the dollar value added to the product or service by the people who work in the operations. This number can then be divided by the number of people, man-hours of work, or dollars of payroll to get productivity measures. This is a complex approach, but some people think it's a valid basis for making comparisons of productivity trends between quite different types of operations.

Value-added measures have the same basic complications as dollarized productivity. In addition, there can be issues about accounting charges and other technicalities. Most of these questions have a small effect on the usefulness of value-added productivity measures used as trends or comparative data.

Proxy Measures

There are various types of proxy measures of productivity. These do not measure productivity directly, but they do provide measures that are likely to be reflective of productivity trends or that correlate with trends in productivity.

One proxy measure is a composite of performance ratings.

Companies that have rated employees' performance in their present positions with a numerical conclusion can calculate the average or median performance for each unit and for the company overall. If these ratings are conducted periodically, a trend of performance can be established, and this change in levels of performance represents a proxy measure of productivity increases or decreases.

Hours of work can be a measure of productivity when the production level or service is constant. Some operations set standards of hours for specified levels of output and then work to better these standards.

A department may measure its effectiveness by the effectiveness of others. Human resources management, for example, might consider company productivity as a proxy effectiveness measure of those who do personnel work.

The Productivity Formula

If one or more of the four basic methods of measuring productivity is not usable for any reason, some type of proxy measure is always possible. Thus the productivity of every organizational unit can be measured in some manner. Remember that the denominator of the productivity equation can always be measured because hours of work can always be counted. If output can't be described and measured, one must ask whether the work of that organizational unit is really necessary.

One way to improve productivity measures is to enhance the understanding of the productivity formula: what we are measuring. There has been a lot of muggy thinking and strange views about productivity. I suggest that you reference the dictionary meaning of productivity.

Conceptually, the productivity formula is very simple: output per man-hour of work. This measures people's effectiveness at work with given products or services as well as existing equipment, supplies, and methods of work. The application of that simple idea is often very complex. We still measure output and man-hours of work. But, as already noted, output means different things in different operations. The denominator of the productivity equation is no longer just a matter of counting hours.

In getting productivity data, you must have a good understanding of the nature of the work performed, the people served, and the critical elements of success. More specifically, I have found it helpful to think of the contemporary productivity formula as follows:

$$P = \frac{\text{Choice} + \text{Quality} + \text{Output} + \text{Errors}}{\text{Number} + \text{Mix} + \text{Type}}$$

In this model, the numerator of the productivity formula has four elements:

1. Choice measures the use of time, doing the right thing.
2. Quality means making a product or providing a service of appropriate high value and dependability.
3. Output is efficiency. This is the number of things produced or services rendered.
4. Errors mean avoiding rework, doing work correctly the first time.

The denominator has three elements:

1. Number is the amount of hours worked by those in the unit being measured.
2. Mix means who did the work and whether that manning represented a good use of scarce talent.
3. Type of work explores what portion of the work is done by the producers.

Getting Productivity Data

Part of effectiveness in productivity management is how good an organization's people are in developing productivity measures. You can be certain that *some* productivity measures can be developed for every organizational unit. With time and experience, you can also be assured that the ability to develop productivity measures will get much better and that the productivity measures will be more useful.

Don't make a big project out of developing productivity measures. Have the managers who know the work the best develop measures of productivity in their own organizations. Start by getting usable productivity measures with the data that is now in your computers. Then make productivity measurement issues an ongoing part of your productivity management activities.

As you work on developing productivity data, remember one important factor: Very few people like to be measured. Measurement identifies failure as well as success. Continuous measurement pushes us to be at our best all of the time. And it is natural to think that measurements never sufficiently reflect the magnitude of our successes or reflect the depth of our efforts.

Some departments and units will argue that they can't develop productivity measures. I have never found that to be true. In fact, as a standard practice, I would offer to develop productivity measures for any unit that said it couldn't be done. I knew it could be done, and I also knew that the unit people would then very quickly develop productivity measures that were better than the ones I had developed.

There are many ways to measure employee productivity. Each has contaminants and imperfections, but there are imperfections in any business data, including personnel data such as turnover and pay data. Such imperfections do not mean that the data are not useful but rather suggest how the data may be used, or, more important, how imperfect data should not be used.

Even imprecise data can serve a useful purpose. Imperfect data used well should be more useful than no data, provided the cost of getting and reporting the data is in line with its value.

A few years ago, there was an instructive case of what can be accomplished in terms of getting usable measures. The management of the Kopper's Company had a commitment to increasing employee productivity for reasons somewhat unique to its own operations. Top management directed every division, every location, every section, and every unit of the company to develop productivity measures, even units such as corporate law.

Rather than embarking on a monumental project with costly

specialists doing the work, management was advised to have the units evolve their own productivity measures, and that's what Kopper's did. There were training sessions and information briefings throughout the company. Cases were developed to illustrate productivity measures. But each unit was charged with the responsibility of developing productivity measures.

As would be expected, there was some complaining and some feeling that "it couldn't be done." Top management persisted, and it *was* done. Productivity measures were developed in every unit of that company within six months.

At Phillips Petroleum a number of years ago, the chief executive officer had an even simpler way of getting productivity measures. The managers of departments that developed approved productivity measures were eligible for annual bonus payments, while others were not. Within a few weeks after that message went out, every department had productivity measures.

I always urge companies to get each organizational unit to develop its own productivity measures. They know their operations the best, so let each unit develop its own productivity data.

Productivity measurements should be made from the bottom up. Focus mostly on measurements for the lowest organizational units at each location. Then these can be combined to get measures of productivity in larger organizational units, and it may be possible to add some additional measures for those larger units.

There are times when productivity data are as valuable in managing as accounting data are. Productivity data are often the only performance measurements at the organizational unit level. Productivity is often an important measurement in nonprofit and government operations, which do not have P&L measures.

To the extent possible, develop productivity measures from data inputted for other purposes, for example, payroll. You may have to record some data especially to calculate important productivity data. An example would be hours of work of exempt persons. Recognize that additional data entries can be a costly and continuing cost. Add as little new data as possible.

Using Productivity Data

As productivity data are developed, it is important to keep in mind how they will be used. Productivity measurements that may seem unacceptable by some mechanical criteria of excellence can be very good data because they are useful in managing.

Even with imperfections, productivity data can be useful. Obviously, there must be an awareness of the imperfection in productivity information. Recognizing the limitations of the productivity data is part of the proper use of any information.

Absolute productivity usually has little value. Productivity data trends plus intracompany and intercompany comparisons of productivity are the most useful. For example, the fact that sales per payroll dollar have a ratio of 3.5 has no significance. But if sales per payroll dollar go to 4.0 (on an index from 100.0 to 114.3), that is very significant.

If comparable operations have a sales per payroll dollar ratio of 3.0, then your operation is 16.7 percent better, and that is significant. And if the sales per payroll dollar of other companies go from 3.0 to 2.8 (100.0 to 93.3) while your operation goes from 100 to 114.3, that is extremely significant.

This simple example makes a very key point. Even if sales per payroll dollar vary significantly, your comparative trend from 100.0 to 122.5 (114.3 divided by 93.3) is still extremely significant.

The main uses of productivity data are for operation measurements, early warning information, and measuring productivity. However, there is a related matter that is important. Businesspeople sometimes say that employees are important assets. The fact of the matter is, however, that employees aren't treated like assets in the various company reporting systems, such as our accounting systems. If employees are assets, for example, shouldn't they be accounted for in some way on the balance sheet? There isn't any number on the asset side of the balance sheet that sets a value on employees. On the company's income statement, employee wages are the only employee-related figure, and they are listed as an expense, according to proper accounting practices.

Productivity data are a measure of employee value and contribution to the success of the company. That corrects a deficiency in accounting, provides proper recognition, and is a very useful business measure.

Performance, Productivity, and Business Results

The development of productivity measures depends in part on an understanding of the relationship between performance, productivity, and operating results. Measures may necessarily be imperfect, but we should be very precise about what it is we are measuring.

Productivity data are partly measures of operating results, but productivity is not the same as business results. Performance is a measure of the effectiveness of individuals or small groups, but performance is not the same as productivity.

Performance is how well a person does his or her job. It is a function of such things as the talent and experience of the person and the degree to which that person does best at work. Productivity relates to the effectiveness of an organizational group. It is the output of an established organizational unit divided by the hours of work of those in that unit. Productivity is essentially performance plus methods of work and capital utilized.

Business results are affected by products and the characteristics of the industry. The results also partly reflect your own company's productivity and the productivity of your competitors. As employee performance increases over a period of time, it's logical that employee productivity should increase and that there should be greater business success. Thus employee productivity is a leading indicator of business results, somewhat like the wholesale price index is an indicator of future consumer prices.

The relationships among performance, productivity, and operating results require deep thought. These relationships differ in various types of activities. However, I suggest that the following are almost always correct in every type of operation:

- Each person and each group will perform at least somewhat better when their performance and their productivity are measured.
- If employee performance increases or if the performance of many employees improves, in the long run, productivity will also inevitably increase.
- Business results and productivity must trend together over a period of time, or one of two things must be true. One possibility is that management made strategic errors with respect to products or markets. The other is that the business changed. If the business has changed, then restart the productivity measures. If management has made

strategic mistakes, then perhaps management must be changed.

+ If productivity improves significantly more in your organization than in your competitor's over a period of time, then you will have business success.
+ Done well, productivity data can measure the excellence of management as well as financial accounting data do.
+ Over a long period of time, productivity must increase as much or more than an index of employee pay.

Basic Productivity Management Action Steps

To this point, we have covered the first four recommended productivity action steps in the EP process. Because these are the essentials, it is worth the time to emphasize them.

In the EP process of productivity management, the first four steps are essential. If they are not adopted in your organization in some appropriate way, you have not used the EP process. You may still have some success in increasing productivity without using these basic four steps—for example, automation and downsizing will increase productivity—but these are one-time events. Some well-known and highly publicized productivity methods do not use at least one of these four steps and the advocates claim success. In every such case I know, the productivity efforts were, in fact, failures.

The EP system may not be the only way to improve productivity, but it is the only method of ongoing productivity management that has proven itself over many years and in hundreds of operations. And in the EP method, these first four steps are absolutely essential.

When these four basic steps are adopted, a very basic productivity management program is in place. These steps may prove to be a sufficient effort. A number of companies do these four steps and nothing else, except on an ad hoc basis in order to deal with special problems, and the productivity of their companies has improved substantially more than the national or industrial rate.

These four steps are required because they are essential

productivity management actions. They are also essential to the success of other productivity steps you might consider, including the eight recommended in the following chapters.

To reiterate, you *must* start the EP method of productivity management by:

1. Gaining an appropriate executive commitment.
2. Starting an effectiveness ethic among employees and all managers of people.
3. Assigning the productivity job to the managers of people.
4. Establishing productivity measures at every level of the organization.

Work hard on these activities, fine-tune each one, and evaluate the results. Only when these basics are being done well should an organization proceed with other productivity management activities.

These first four steps are a manageable job in most organizations. It is a great advantage to be able to take on the productivity management job in manageable steps.

Recognize that this is a process that can be used in any size company and in any type of activity. It is a process that can be used in any section of any company, even the smallest unit.

Productivity management isn't free, but it is almost free when you take the first four steps. The amount of *extra* time required to implement them is so small that it would be hard to measure. The only certain cash expenditure in these basic four steps is the price of this book. In these first steps, you will need little additional outside help, and probably none at all.

6

Utilizing Technology

Throughout economic history, productivity improvement has mostly resulted from capital substitution. This is still true, and future productivity improvement will largely depend upon success in substituting capital for man-hours of work.

Capital substitution should thus be an important action step to consider in any productivity improvement method. It is action step 5 in the EP process of productivity management, following implementation of the four required basic action steps discussed in Chapters 2 through 5.

Capital substitution is not a required step in the EP process. Some companies are now utilizing technology for productivity improvement about as well as they can. But for every organization, the utilization of technology should be considered. For many companies, utilizing technology will be the most important method of increasing productivity. In fact, for some organizations, the potential for a productivity gain from capital substitution is greater than from all other productivity action steps combined.

Important changes are occurring in use of technology and capital substitution in productivity management. Understanding these changes is critical to the proper use of technology in effectively substituting machine power for human effort.

Historically, substituting capital for labor has, in effect, largely been a centralized purchasing activity. Productivity improvement still involves purchasing equipment to replace human effort. Increasingly, however, there are more purchasing decisions to be made and more people who make these purchasing decisions, and many of the capital substitution decisions are made by people throughout the organization. Some of the new machines substitute for mental activities as well as for physical work. This adds another whole new dimension to productivity improvement.

Perhaps most important is the fact that the workers control the output of the new machines in an increasing number of cases. The latitude granted to workers to use some of the new machines means that how they use them affects productivity improvement resulting from capital substitution.

Although capital substitution for some organizations may be, as stated earlier, the most important method of increasing productivity, this is one of the shortest chapters in this book. The great importance of capital substitution and the dearth of information and recommendations about how to utilize such machines as computers to increase productivity reflect a major problem. This suggests that work needs to be done to learn how to use the new technologies better.

Purchasing Productivity

In the past, most of the productivity achieved by capital substitution was a centralized purchasing activity by experts in the corporate headquarters. Generally, engineers and methods experts used scientific methods in some way to determine the cost effectiveness of substituting capital for human effort. As long as the payroll savings were distinctly more than the cost of the equipment purchased, a company would buy all the machinery it could finance.

Since the 1920s, most of the machines purchased to substitute for labor were in factories and warehouses. Companies mechanized and automated production and storage facilities. Most of the equipment purchased to increase productivity was special purpose and, once installed, all employees essentially used the machines in the same way. The machines controlled the pace of work as well as the method of work.

That type of capital substitution still goes on and is an

important part of productivity management work in many companies. Substituting machines for human effort in factories, warehouses, and transportation will likely contribute as much to productivity improvement in the foreseeable future as it did in the past. Starting in the 1950s, however, a new generation of machines emerged and is now an increasingly important part of capital substitution. These machines are mostly computers, communications equipment, and office machines. They are used everywhere in the organization.

Many of the machines now being substituted for human effort are still purchased in the same basic centralized manner. An example is the mainframe computer for payroll work. Equipment such as mainframe computers has mostly been purchased by large organizations that have their own experts in MIS and scientific management. The buyers can also use such consulting firms as EDS or one of the big six accounting firms to help them in this work. Companies like EDS will even operate these large-scale information systems on a contract basis after they are installed.

Larger organizations are now also buying equipment systems on a centralized basis to store and handle information and files on a grand scale. The information of a large file department can be reduced to a few discs and accessed very quickly. Think of it this way: First we used machines to replace bookkeepers, and now we're using machines to replace file clerks.

The possible applications of these large computer systems to replace human effort have not been exhausted. There are many areas of work in large companies where computer systems have not yet been used to replace manpower. Wherever there are many man-hours of work, involving highly repetitive tasks, there is a potential for a large-scale system application to substitute machine effort for man-hours. The suppliers of computer equipment will continue to seek new opportunities to develop equipment to replace human effort.

The mainframes and other equipment that make it possible to use machines instead of people are getting better, faster, and cheaper. The people they replace are just getting more expensive. There is now better equipment and better software, so large systems applications put in place even a few years ago can be upgraded. There is a replacement market for productivity machines involving billions of dollars in sales. Many large companies that were the early buyers of computers for work such are payroll are targets for further productivity improvement by upgrading their equipment.

As long as the payroll savings are distinctly higher than the depreciated cost of the equipment and the cost of financing, companies will continue to use systems applications that substitute equipment for man-hours on a large scale. Systems applications in computer work also are being increasingly implemented in small companies, where the system can be handled by PCs instead of mainframes. However, the work still reflects systems developed for a broad class of work such as payroll. These general systems applications will continue as far into the future as we can plan. They represent a source for a great potential productivity gain in the future.

Dispersed Purchasing of Some Machines and Software

Increasingly, the machines being purchased to substitute for human effort are used by individuals and organizational units. These machines represent part of the equipment, facilities, and materials of organizational units. At least in part, the decisions about purchasing these machines must be made by the operating managers throughout the organization, which means that the operating managers must be accountable for purchasing PCs and copiers and software, just as they would be accountable for purchasing desks and calculators. All such purchases, of course, are subject to the organization's budget and operational control processes.

This new equipment is generally low in cost compared to the man-hours replaced. Because the cost and the risk of error are moderate, it makes sense to have the individual manager, who knows the work and knows what would increase work effectiveness, be responsible for purchases rather than the large and expensive central decision-making groups who do not know the operations well.

Some companies have concerns that managers might make

purchasing mistakes, particularly because of the technology involved. Of course, that is correct. However, managers may make
mistakes about any part of their job. With respect to computers,
for instance, the operating manager can usually get advice from
computer experts and is subject to guidance by higher level
managers.

Consider this also: Mistakes made by managers about machine purchases affect only their own organization. Centralized
purchasing mistakes apply to all departments.

Using Machines

A lot of the equipment to be purchased by managers is worker-
controlled. This means that the workers have opportunities to use
the machines well or not use them well. How well they use these
new machines is becoming a more important element of productivity management. Now, productivity by machine substitution
means getting the right equipment to substitute for human effort
and using that equipment correctly.

The latitude in the use of the machines may be very great.
When that is the case, proper use may be more important than
having the best machines. Latitude in the use of these machines
complicates decisions about buying the equipment. How well the
machines will be used must be considered in purchasing decisions. This usually means that affirmative productivity decisions
must generally have a much greater margin between greater
output and the cost of the application.

Even in simple work using PCs, such as word processing,
the operator has many choices in using the equipment. As you
get into more complex uses of computers, the latitude in the use
of these machines can be very great.

Using the machines properly is a matter of capability with
the equipment and the desire to use it to work more productively.
Workers must then have qualifications *and* a striving for excellence.

As an organization introduces productivity machines, there
is often a need for retraining and practical behavioral modification. Workers must have know-how. And perhaps for the first

time, workers must also have an effectiveness ethic and an inclination to take the initiative for an improvement in productivity.

These are productivity machines. They can increase productivity in office and administrative work enormously. Or operators can spend time doing interesting things with the machines. These machines can be tools or toys. Some workers become addicted to the machines. Sometimes employees use PCs as a computer game.

Keep in mind that there are many people who operate these machines in an organization. Some use the machines only occasionally, but there are many who use them. It is this widespread usage, as well as the great leverage for more highly productive work or wasted time, that makes proper use such a critical issue in productivity management.

Decisions regarding the use of the machines and the software can be made only by the operator-worker and that worker's immediate supervising manager. This is another reason why decisions about dispersed productivity work must be delegated to the managers. They must decide to empower the workers to use the machines or decide not to empower them, depending on how skillful each worker is in their use and each worker's inclination to use them to achieve a higher effectiveness of work.

The machines can provide guidance to the operator with respect to use, either from expert systems or programmed instructions. Equipment manufacturers and MIS professionals are striving to make these machines easier to use. Even with such improvements, worker-controlled output must be managed by the immediate manager.

We are still near the bottom of the learning curve in managing the use of productivity machines. Better machines are coming on the market as fast as we can learn how to use them. The new machines generally create a broader latitude for use and, therefore, more skillful monitoring and management of how these machines should be used are critical to achieving high levels of work excellence.

Expanding the Mind

As the productivity machines are dispersed throughout the organization and become more worker-controlled, these machines are likely to affect mental capability as well as reduce man-hours. This is a new facet of productivity management, with enormous potential for increasing effectiveness.

In considering the effect of computers on mental work, some people emphasize how computers, calculators, and other office machines save workers' time. These machines can't think, but they can remember, compute, copy, and analyze. With them, workers can perform activities and tasks much more efficiently and, therefore, save a great deal of time. This reduces man-hours of work and increases productivity.

I also emphasize the ability of the machines to expand the mind. The machines make work possible that could otherwise not be done, or they make far more effective work possible. Then you don't reduce the denominator of the productivity equation; in fact, man-hours of work might increase. But this use of productivity machines increases output.

There are limits to reducing man-hours in any organization. Once you have a workerless operation, you can't reduce man-hours at all. And, of course, a practical minimum or threshold of employees is needed. If nothing else, man-hours are required to operate and maintain the machines.

When machines expand the mind, however, there is no practical limit on productivity improvement. As far as we know, there are no limits on intelligence or the excellence of thinking.

There are many well-known cases of productivity machines expanding the mind. CAD and CAP are two widely used examples. The effect of both on employee productivity has been enormous.

The experts tell us that there are many opportunities to apply machines more effectively by the use of expert systems, simple modeling, and interactive computer systems. Each of these activities helps workers use the equipment for more activities and does the work better and quicker. If you use a computer in your work, or if you might use one, the interactive use of this equipment might support greater work effectiveness.

Don't assume that increasing productivity through the more effective use of mental capabilities is done only by knowledge workers and top-level professionals. The highest levels of knowledge workers and professionals have the greatest opportunities to increase productivity by expanding the mind, but many other workers in lower level jobs also have this opportunity. Empowered workers and managers who have been delegated the productivity improvement job are the ones most likely to bring about the effective use of machines to increase or expand mental capability in a way that reflects itself in higher productivity. Only in a workplace with a productivity culture are such productivity increases likely to occur.

Not much has been written about productivity and the use of machines to expand the mind. That's partly because the experts deal almost exclusively with broadly applicable systems and methods that replace workers and reduce man-hours of work.

I would urge you not to emphasize increasing productivity by the effective use of mental capability in the early phases of productivity management work. I think using computers to expand the mind is something that will happen, but it will happen one employee at a time and cannot be forced. The important thing is to have a productivity improvement system that facilitates and encourages the use of computers to increase mental capability, and the EP process does that.

Advice and Support

To deal with the centralized purchasing of large-scale computer applications requires the highest level of technical and professional knowledge in the computer field. These decisions are made at the highest executive management level of the company. These are important decisions involving substantial amounts of money. Errors can be very costly. A company must be a very careful and prudent buyer. Major systems applications decisions are business investment decisions. The issue is whether a company should invest funds in equipment to replace man-hours, or whether the funds should be invested in other activities. Large-scale computer applications involve purchasing equipment to improve productivity and lower costs. Executives are essentially buying productivity. The whole process of buying major computer applications is outside the EP process of productivity improvement, or any other productivity improvement effort that I know of.

The EP method of productivity management requires that operating managers have the job of increasing effectiveness and assumes that they will get whatever support is needed to do this job. Nowhere do operating managers need more support than in utilizing technology. Over the years, companies have tried to provide needed advice and support to managers in the dispersed buying of capital equipment to substitute for human effort and in the use of the technology machines. Following are some ideas and recommendations.

I urge that managers be more insistent about choosing software, or prescribing very specifically what the software should be able to do. When the task is the same throughout the company, the software should be the same. For example, for the same task, WordPerfect might be used throughout a company. But where the work is unique to an operation, the operating manager must have the authority to select the software.

Be reasonable about issues like the integrity of the mainframe and privacy. There is so much at stake with the mainframe systems that they must be immunized from all PC systems. So I would urge you always to be inclined to concede issues relating to the integrity of the mainframe systems.

Privacy and secrecy are other matters. With computers and the communications equipment of today and tomorrow, the fact is that there will be a much more open work environment. There won't be many secrets. There must be fewer reasons for keeping secrets and reasonable ground rules for "right to know" information. Productivity cannot be restrained by the potential misuse of information.

There is an enormous amount of equipment and software for sale, and those who offer these products can be very good salespersons. Operating managers and empowered employees are not experienced buyers. These considerations suggest the need to do some training on purchase procedures and to set up screens to help managers with these decisions.

Be very careful about any software that requires changing operating practices, adding information that is not kept at the present time, or changing the information you now use. All of these changes are extremely costly and often serve the needs of the software provider, not your organization.

The essential problem in utilizing equipment is that the machines and software experts focus their attention on equipment excellence. Efforts are being made to make the technology easier to use, but the focus is still on technical excellence. Unfortunately, the experts haven't taken the time to tell any individual or group how to use the technology.

Workers and managers know their work and the specifics of how that work is done. But the workers often know so little about the technology that they don't try to use it to improve the effectiveness of their work. One way to break this dilemma is by training workers in how to use the technology. The training needed is not for established software but how to use it for special tasks and activities. There is a great need for training people in how to use these productivity machines. Push your training department to do good work in this area.

With or without a training department effort, I urge organizations to develop coaching and mentoring activities. Some managers and employees are far more adept in using computer technology than others. Share the knowledge that resides in the organization about how to utilize technology to improve productivity. You might even consider having a hot line for help in using different equipment and software. Have these inside your organization to the extent possible.

Consider establishing an internal consulting capability in the use of technology for increasing productivity. In my opinion, any organization with more than about fifty employees should have such a capability. The person or persons who provide this in-house capability in the use of technology should be available for assistance and advice. This would not be a productivity department but individuals who are particularly good in utilizing technology for productivity improvement and who spend part of their time doing this work. These people will become more expert with time and with each case they work on.

When there is an especially difficult case in utilizing technology, or when there is a case affecting a number of jobs, consider setting up a project group to deal with that specific case. Include in that group the operating managers involved and the in-house experts. Have very specific objectives and when they are achieved, or when it is clear that they will not be achieved, discontinue the group's work. Remember: There should be no separate productivity organizations.

When operating managers have been given the responsibility of dispersed buying, they will find more ways to utilize these technologies. Consider other methods when they are clearly needed, but continue to place the basic accountability for using technology with the operating managers.

7

Unproductive Practices

Action step 6 is to remove unproductive practices of all types. There probably isn't any organization that could not improve the effectiveness of work at least somewhat by removing unproductive practices. In some cases an organization will judge that there are few unproductive practices or that the time and cost of removing the ones that exist make this productivity action step impractical. Some organizations will recognize this step as being politically sensitive and will either avoid it or just eliminate some of the practices.

Removing unproductive practices is a postponable step. There is generally no clear point in time when you should proceed. It is also possible to remove unproductive practices over a period of time, thereby avoiding a major effort or major confrontations. However you do it, consider increasing productivity in this manner.

Attack Unproductive Practices

Consider launching a vendetta against unproductive practices of all types anywhere in the organization and at every level. Plan to be aggressive. Wage a war against unproductive practices.

If an organization has never tried to remove unproductive practices, the chances are that productivity can be improved by as much as 10 percent through this step alone. New unproductive practices can deter productivity increases by as much as 1 to 2 percent a year, so there is a need for an assault on unproductive practices every three to five years.

Work on removing unproductive practices can encounter serious opposition. Many such practices were thought to be useful or necessary by someone, at some time, for some reason. Some people might still think that these practices are useful, or they might be defensive.

Unproductive practices represent someone's work and may involve some jobs. Perhaps top-level people with power and sensitive feelings sponsored the practice you now want to eliminate. These are some of the things you might encounter when you try to remove unproductive practices.

No matter what the resistance is or who the opponents are, set out to remove every unproductive practice. Be an evangelist about removing unproductive practices, because you know the value of greater productivity and are confident that the high moral ground is always productive activity versus nonproductive activity.

Unproductive practices can be a cancer that will detract from or corrupt productive activities and effective workers. Unproductive practices use excessive time and may cause others extra work also. Such practices detract from productivity work in indirect ways. For example, unproductive practices detract from a productivity culture, or they may be copied and become a standard of work.

There may be good reasons why some unproductive practices evolved, or someone thought there were good reasons. For example, make-work rules in a factory may have been a reaction to past management practices. Increasingly, some unproductive practices are also thought to be helpful in defending possible compliance issues. Whatever someone's good intentions, work relentlessly to remove every unproductive practice.

Some people confuse activity and effort with work. They may think that being busy and being productive are the same thing, and they defend unproductive practices because people seem to be working hard. Some also urge unproductive practices because they think some activity enhances the quality of work life, or serves some other social or psychological goal. Whatever the purpose, unproductive practices have a cost, and that must also be considered. One cost is lower productivity.

Push hard for the elimination of unproductive practices even when the opposition reflects good intentions or noble causes. High productivity and higher living standards for working people are noble causes, too.

Special Targets

Attack special unproductive practices, which I call productivity viruses. Six major productivity viruses common to many companies are:

Informania
Interference
Courtesy work
Meetings
Travel
Multiple management

Informania is the latest major time killer. There has been a lot of talk about computer viruses, but the biggest computer virus of all is informania, or collecting information because the computer can handle it. Informania means working with the computer because it is interesting rather than because it is productive. It means bigger but not better reports because of the capacity of the machine rather than the needs of those who receive the material.

A widespread productivity virus involves *interference*. United Airlines once made the front page of *Business Week* because all of its executives met first thing each morning to view routes, schedules, and available planes on a massive computer display in a room especially designed for that purpose. Imagine top executives doing low-level scheduling as a group, and every morning! The executives were interfering with the work of the schedulers. There is a lot of interference in organizations, and some of it is from the top.

Some people have encouraged interference under the banner of participation. A participant may think that his or her involvement and suggestions are useful, but the person affected will often think that it is interference. Whatever the view, the result is lower productivity.

It is always nice to be courteous, but dig out and eliminate *courtesy work*. This would include inviting people to a meeting out of courtesy because their feelings might be hurt otherwise, even though they had nothing to contribute and were not really involved.

Meetings are useful for a limited number of purposes, mostly to give and receive information. Meetings are also sometimes a good way to get input from different people with appropriate backgrounds. Many meetings are none of the above and are just a waste of time. Some meetings are an escape from work.

Work hard to eliminate unnecessary meetings. Check the length of the meetings. Make sure that they are run productively.

When I was doing a lot of work for the Aetna Insurance Company in Hartford, Connecticut, most of the senior managers scheduled meetings an hour before lunch and late on Friday afternoons. There were few long meetings at Aetna. It worked like magic.

When Frank Pace was chairman of the compensation committee at Time, he ran meetings as he did in the army. Most people were scheduled. I was usually given exactly one hour. When your time was up, you were politely stopped and ushered out. It worked on me. My three-hour presentations were made in fifty-nine minutes and thirty seconds.

Being a consultant, I caused a lot of meetings. Many of those meetings I held were not needed, were usually much too long, and almost always were attended by people who had no real reason for being there.

As a consultant, I also had to *travel* a lot for many years. But very early, I realized how much time I wasted going to and from the plane, on the plane, and at the hotel. My answer was that I took my secretary-assistant on every trip when I was running Sibson & Company. Many commented on how much I got done on my trips, but I can assure you that it increased my productivity enormously.

It may not be practical for every company to have people travel as couples, but most companies could cut down on travel.

It isn't really the cost of the travel as much as it is the waste of time. Travel is a major target of opportunity for eliminating unproductive practices. Work hard to eliminate trips or make better use of your time when you are traveling.

Multiple management has long been a special target of opportunity in eliminating unproductive practices. This used to mean committees and collective bargaining. Now, scaling back on multiple management is also related to ombudsmen, quality circles, total quality management, projects groups, and teams of various types.

I have long argued that the only committees that should exist are the committees of the board. I exaggerated slightly to make a necessary point, but some companies are mired in a web of committees. What is so amazing is programs that set out to increase productivity by establishing another organization and, therefore, a multiple management system. Companies already have one organization that is unproductive enough. Now those who say they have a way to increase quality and effectiveness start out by adding another ineffective organization, which detracts from effectiveness even more. That's like taking another drink to sober up.

Another form of multiple management involves teams. Some urge teams as a method of increasing productivity or quality. In every case I know, teams detract from productivity. They may be necessary for one reason or another, but using them is usually an unproductive practice.

Sometimes teams are little more than temporary project groups. Sometimes they are self-directed work groups. But if these teams represent multiple management, they tend to detract from productivity. Each team overlaps the organization of the company, and they often overlap each other. This can be a path to organizational anarchy and chaos. Whatever good may be said about the team concept, teams result in multiple management and usually tend to lower productivity.

There will be other unproductive practices to attack in your own organization. The six identified here exist in almost every organization and represent a good place to start. After you have had experience with such practices, you will become more expert in identifying and eliminating the unproductive practices that are unique to your own organization.

Obsolete Practices

An important part of the effective management of change is dealing with obsolescence in a timely and effective manner. In an era of rapid change, which is mostly driven by technology, the life cycle of best practices is often only a few years. The productive operation must be alert to obsolescence and must be willing to eliminate or modify obsolete practices.

The problem with obsolete practices and programs is that the obsolescence happens a little at a time and over a period of time. That means that there is rarely a clear point in time when someone should take a stand and say, "No more," and determine to get rid of obsolete programs. Another problem is that these programs take on a life of their own. The bigger the program, the more likely it will develop a life of its own and a tendency to survive efforts to eliminate it.

A big program requires special skill in administration and involves many man-hours. Those who know how to run the program and those who are paid to administer it have reasons to keep it. Furthermore, with time, a program becomes the company way and a company tradition. All of those things mean that programs and practices have great staying power, even when they are obsolete.

Obsolete programs aren't always inoperative or useless. They are obsolete in the sense that they don't work well anymore. The comparison I make is with airplanes. The old DC-6 is obsolete. It still flies across the country, but a 747 can carry three times as many people the same distance in less than half the time. That means that the 747 is about six times as productive and the old DC-6 is obsolete.

There are many obsolete programs in every area of an organization. Take the compensation area. When I wrote the fifth edition of *Compensation*,* the following compensation practices

*Robert E. Sibson, *Compensation*, AMACOM, New York, 1990.

had become obsolete in varying degrees: job descriptions, job evaluation, surveying, salary increase budgets, merit salary systems, and traditional termination pay practices based on years of service. But these six items represented two-thirds of the contents of the first edition, which was published in 1960.

Based on a survey of compensation practices made in 1992, four of five companies had at least three of the six obsolete practices I listed. One in five companies still had all six obsolete practices. Amazingly, at the time the survey was conducted, a few companies were implementing at least one of these obsolete plans for the first time.

The compensation field is not unique. The degree of obsolescence described above is typical in most areas of work in most organizations.

Over the many years that I worked for Itek Corporation, that company dealt with obsolescence by putting sunset dates on each program. These were dates when the programs had to be reviewed or automatically cancelled. Management wasn't rigid about the review beyond that the program had to be reconsidered and a determination made about whether it was still appropriate or should be modified. If a change had to be made, Itek didn't insist that it be made on the sunset date, only that some type of a plan for change had to be made at that time. That's one way of dealing with obsolete practices. However you do it, recognize that obsolete practices are unproductive practices and detract from productivity.

Deregulating the Organization

Bureaucracy is its own form of an unproductive practice. Generally speaking, productivity will be increased if bureaucratic practices can be eliminated.

Bureaucrats are unproductive. They produce nothing, but their man-hours must be counted in the denominator of the productivity equation. Bureaucratic practices involve required steps and procedures. These add to hours of work but rarely add to effectiveness. Regulated work and bureaucratic practices exist in part to avoid mistakes, to make sure that things are not done incorrectly. But that is a very negative work environment and is not conducive to work excellence.

Bureaucrats seek to avoid mistakes by having work done one way. But uniform work methods are *designed* to be unproductive. A uniform work method must be designed so everyone can do the work in the prescribed manner. That means that the work system must be designed so the least talented and the least effective workers can do the assigned tasks in a prescribed manner. By design, this means that unproductive work is imposed on more effective workers.

In high-technology work, the regulators lack an understanding of the work that is done. There is then no realistic way for bureaucrats to prescribe methods of work or sensible controls, and the imposed bureaucratic methods are essentially administrative. Administrative regulations not only cause unproductive work, but they may retard the application of technology as well.

Some think that bureaucratic methods are needed to ensure a high quality of work and customer satisfaction. My experience suggests that bureaucratic methods of management cause people to look inward, not outward, and result in uniform mediocrity.

Whatever arguments there are for bureaucracy, one result is that the regulators retain power centrally. Whether based on a lack of confidence in lower level managers or a lack of confidence in working people, regulations and bureaucratic practices involve controlling work from the top. This is the opposite of delegative management processes, and in that sense they may also impede productivity improvement actions throughout the organization.

Finally, bureaucratic rules and practices create their own work. The rules must be written, communicated, and enforced. All of this requires time and probably does not mean higher output. Then productivity will be lower because the output isn't greater, but the hours of work are.

Productivity Bargaining

The proportion of the workforce represented by unions has declined steadily for the past twenty years and is now only about 12 percent of the private workforce. But in operations that have unions, there are still work rules that depress productivity as well as a considerable amount of featherbedding. These are unproductive practices, and they must be eliminated by productivity bargaining.

There may be reasons why these work rules and featherbedding exist. Some restrictive work rules exist because of former management practices or because of questions about safety. Some restrictive work rules exist because they require more workers and that means more union members. Some restrictive work rules exist to make work easier. Before you start productivity bargaining, try to understand the possible causes for restrictive work rules in union contracts.

Productivity bargaining mostly means eliminating every work rule, restrictive practice, and featherbedding provision. Productivity bargaining should also involve affirmative negotiations to find methods of increasing productivity. But productivity bargaining doesn't mean getting the union to participate in management. Productivity bargaining means getting the union to agree to productive work.

I have often urged an approach to collective bargaining that started with an identification of some essentials for a collective bargaining relationship. These were nonnegotiable issues. The company had some and recognized that the union would have some also.

I think there are three essentials in collective bargaining for the employer: productive work, competitive levels of pay, and the elimination of adversarial roles. A company should do everything necessary and legal to get these three things in collective bargaining. Managers should also focus on these essentials in the course of their day-to-day work under a labor contract. If productivity bargaining fails, go after decertification. If that fails too, do whatever else is necessary to get a productive workforce, competitive pay, and a cooperative, positive work environment, including bankruptcy. That's not being antiunion; it's being pro-productivity and pro-worker.

Workers favor productive work. Union workers favor high productivity and productivity bargaining even when their union representatives don't. Union and nonunion employees clearly think that unions have been wrong in not giving their full support to productivity improvement efforts.

The following findings are based on my 1992 study of the views of American workers on employee-employer relationships:*

* The overwhelming majority of workers think that unions once had a valuable role to play, but that this is no longer the case, mostly because unions have not supported competitive pay and productive work practices.
* Four of five workers think unions should support efforts to increase productivity.
* Four of five workers think work rules are a major reason why so many good paying jobs have been lost to overseas workers.

Unneeded Work, Goofing Off, and Trivial Pursuit

There are a lot of make-work practices and featherbedding provisions in nonunion operations as well. There are unproductive practices in high-level as well as low-level jobs. Make-work practices exist in every area of an operation.

Some unproductive work is just part of working. Some days are better than others; some activities go better than others. There is some goofing off everywhere at work. We have all done some of that. That's part of work. No one can work their hardest and with optimum effectiveness at every task and all the time.

In work controlled by machines or by the flow of work, wasted time may be minimal. But in most jobs, some unneeded work and some degree of wasted time are inevitable. If maximum effectiveness all the time is 100 percent, then the optimum practical effectiveness in most jobs is probably no more than 90 percent.

When employees do unneeded work, it is unproductive work because it wastes precious time. When higher level managers waste time, this also trivializes work effectiveness. I report here only negative cases that have been published by the company or where I have the company's permission to do so.

*See Appendix B.

A case of trivial pursuit came to light recently about the executives of Hyatt Hotels. According to information published by the company's vice president of human resources, the 400 or so people in corporate headquarters spend time doing the work of low-level hotel workers. They even have a word for it: in-touch day. A picture was published of the president of the company putting luggage into the trunk of a car in front of one of their hotels.

The rationale for this action was that the president would be able to learn the business, we hope without getting a hernia. One would think that the president had put baggage into a car before, that he had learned the hotel business prior to becoming president, and that he would be spending a lot of time in the hotels while doing his own job.

Other "blue chip" companies engage in similar workplace activities. You should hope that you never get a hamburger prepared by a McDonald's executive.

There are many cases of trivial pursuit at work, with the trend more in higher level jobs because there is more discretion in the use of time. There is also more trivial pursuit in very profitable companies and in organizations like government that have no accountability for results.

Identify and eliminate unneeded work. The worst of all productivity possibilities is to work hard and effectively on the wrong things or on unneeded activities. Unneeded work is wasteful and unproductive. Unproductive work often requires work by others, and this leverages unproductiveness. Unneeded work is "disproductivity" when the unneeded work done by one person causes others to do work that is also unneeded.

High productivity requires doing needed work and doing it to the best of one's ability. High productivity requires personal effort.

Never forget productivity's little secret: You must work hard to be productive. Work is often difficult and tiring, and it takes a substantial effort to work hard enough.

Managing Unproductive Practices

Productivity has often been associated with efficiency experts and firms that are hired to eliminate jobs. Some of the consultants who do that work guarantee results, and some of them even base their fees on the reduction in payroll that results from their work.

What these firms mostly do is look for unproductive practices, and some of the better ones are very good at it. None of the sacred cows in the client company are theirs, so these consultants can get rid of the unproductive work and eliminate jobs. Mostly, though, they do this by eliminating the types of unproductive practices described in this chapter.

They are safe in guaranteeing results. Every company has some unproductive practices, and some companies have a lot of them. On average, if the work is done by tough-minded people, eliminating 5 percent of payroll is a walk in the park. In an assignment for a company with 500 employees, if an efficiency expert firm negotiated a fee of 5 percent of payroll savings, the fee might work out to be more than $200,000. A job like that could be done mostly by intermediate-level professionals in less 400 hours. That means a pretty fancy fee for work that a company could do for itself if it had the will.

An important part of managing unproductive practices is to manage time effectively. It isn't a simple matter of unproductive or productive practices. There are many gradations. For example, part of the job of managing time is to manage the use of time in some proportion to the importance of what is done.

Another action step that is sometimes used, particularly in high-tech companies, is managing knowledge, which is also an increasingly important subject of managing. A great deal of knowledge work involves doing the right thing and that includes eliminating unneeded work.

Many special interest groups cause unproductive practices, and in order to have high productivity, companies must handle these groups well. Dealing with special interest groups takes time and that depresses productivity. If the special interest group is successful in getting preferential treatment for its constituents, then less qualified people may be given work assignments. Aside from the question of fairness, assigning less qualified people to work will very likely reduce employee productivity.

You might think that preferential treatment for some group and discrimination in their favor is the correct social thing to do. If this is the case, recognize that there is a cost for favored treatment, and the cost is often in the form of unproductive practices and lower productivity.

There are two related aspects of compliance and unproductive practices. These relate to the concept of work contamination and zero-risk management practices. Both create or support unproductive practices.

Work contamination has to do with the effect of unproductive workers on productive workers. If you have a group of workers with different levels of effectiveness, they will, if left alone, tend to work toward the level of the least productive. In order to have high levels of productivity, you must bring the work of everyone up to the level of the most effective workers in the group by various management methods. That's the job of the operating managers.

Too often, unnecessary loss of productivity related to special interest groups and compliance is initiated by the employer. For example, laws are passed and the lawyers and consultants get employers to do all sorts of costly things to defend themselves against possible actions by activists and compliance officials. The efforts are often to avoid taking a risk: zero-risk management. Huge costs can result from zero-risk management, most of which relate to unproductive practices.

If unproductive practices are a productivity action step that your organization is considering, there is the question of how to proceed. There are three possibilities: hire an efficiency expert, have a central management engineering staff organization, or trust the operating managers to do the job. And, of course, a company can do any two or all of these three things.

I have advised a number of clients to hire an expert in this field. I did so when all of the following conditions were met:

- The company had not used an efficiency expert for at least ten years.
- There were more than six organizational levels in the company.
- The company doubled the proportion of staff and support jobs during the past twenty years.
- The personnel ratio was 1.0 percent or more, and other

staff organizations had equivalent levels of staff organizations.

I would generally recommend a central management engineering activity in any company with more than 200 jobs (not people). However, this would be a central advisory function. This function should be set up in an existing organization, preferably in a management engineering activity or personnel.

For all companies and under all circumstances, it is the operating managers who are able to manage unproductive practices the best. There isn't any better way. You need capable managers who have been delegated the authority to manage. Consultants and management engineering professionals may assist and support the productivity management work of the operating managers, but they can never take the place of the operating managers.

The point must be made again and again that it is the operating manager who mostly does the productivity management job. It must be said repeatedly because the role of the operating manager is critical in so much productivity improvement work.

8

Empowerment

Empowerment, productivity action step 7, means to give power or authority, or to authorize. Empowerment at work mostly means giving workers *more* authority to determine work methods. When workers have knowledge that is critical to effective work and that knowledge is not possessed by management, empowerment can be an important productivity management action step to consider.

The basic concepts and practices of empowerment are not new. As far back as 1950, forces related to technology started to require more and more empowerment. My first experience with it was in 1952. I first reported delegative management and empowerment in *The Sibson Report* in 1982. Increasing technology and a greater need to be competitive are focusing more attention on empowerment and making this an increasingly important productivity action step.

Whenever empowerment is part of a productivity improvement effort, it is important to make sure that all managers and workers know what empowerment is, as well as its limits. This usually requires some type of a briefing.

Briefing on Empowerment

Delegative management refers specifically to granting authority for making all types of decisions to the managers of people.

Empowerment refers to the delegation of authority by the managers to each worker, mostly with respect to work practices and methods. When there is empowerment, workers at every level are empowered to act, not just make suggestions. Under empowerment, this authority to act is limited to the worker's own job, not to the work practices of others.

The delegation of authority from the manager of personnel to each worker empowers each worker to determine at least some work methods and practices without prior review. The worker then has important elements of authority to determine the best way to do the job that has been assigned.

Empowerment is such a simple idea. It means granting latitude of action for how the work is done to those who do the work. The employee will often know something about the work and how it can best be done that no one else knows. Empowerment uses that knowledge to optimize productivity and work excellence.

When workers are granted authority to determine work methods, they are *managing,* and in some limited sense, they are managers. The management of work that is inherent in empowerment includes the responsibility for effective work. Thus when there is true empowerment, each employees is directly and personally involved in productivity management.

Delegation to managers and the empowerment of workers are not intellectual games or academic exercises. With increasing technology, there is clearly more of a need for decisions to be made where the technologies are known and that is more often with the employees who do the work. Furthermore, with more worker-controlled machines, the knowledge of how to use the equipment increasingly resides with those who use it.

Obviously, empowerment works better in some jobs than in others. Empowerment contributes to greater productivity the most when workers' knowledge is important to the work, when machines used in the work are worker-controlled, and when work methods are not inherently prescribed. These conditions exist in more and more jobs in an era of technology, and except in highly automated plants, they exist to some degree in all jobs.

It is important always to recognize that the nature of the operations will very much affect the degree of delegation and the specific practices used to achieve delegation and empowerment. My favorite example of how empowerment is influenced by the operations is TRW. The company's operations in Ohio (TRW East) are mostly manufacturing facilities for automobile parts. They are highly automated and highly unionized. In this environment, only a limited amount of empowerment is possible. TRW on the West Coast (TRW West) is involved in high-tech electronics operations with no unions and extreme degrees of empowerment, which are essential for effective operations.

Empowerment is partly a style of management. Therefore, you should not consider it as an action step in productivity work unless the more basic decisions relating to a more delegative style of management have been made by top management and that style exists throughout the organization. Specifically, empowerment will not work in an organization that has a centralized or bureaucratic style of management. Such organizations can do some participation and involvement but not empowerment.

As stated earlier, the delegation of responsibility for productivity improvement should go through management levels to every worker in the company. It is an error to talk about "the company" empowering workers. Each level of management delegates to the next level of management, and at each level of the organization, managers empower nonmanagers who are direct-reports.

Don't ever think that empowerment dilutes or diminishes the job of the manager any more than delegation to managers dilutes or diminishes the job of executive management. There is nothing about this action step that conflicts with action step 3: assigning the productivity management job to the operating managers. Clearly, however, empowerment changes the job of employees, managers, and executives in terms of what is done and how it is done.

People have a better understanding of the work methods they determine. That's a powerful argument for empowerment.

Rapid change often comes with high technology. Rapid change requires a quicker reaction capability. The ability to react the quickest is usually with those who do the work. Empowerment thus facilitates high productivity in an environment of rapid change.

Whenever employees know things about their work that others don't know, there is another reason for empowerment. Those who know the work the best are likely to have ideas for improving productivity that others would not have. They should be able to act to improve productivity, not just suggest ways the work can be done better.

It may be possible to get the information from those who possess it and then use that knowledge to help determine what those workers are told to do. That's exactly what companies sometimes do in participative management processes. That approach doesn't work very well for very long. Employees may have ideas about how others might be able to do their work better and that should be encouraged but not imposed. Each worker must be empowered to accept or not accept the ideas of others.

Don't ever delegate authority to interfere or intrude in the work of others. Some participative systems do that, partly to get peer pressure for better work. I have never seen authority to interfere with the work of others that hasn't caused controversy and divisiveness.

Workers' jobs change dramatically when there is empowerment. As noted earlier, a job that has authority to determine work methods has at least the elements of management. Empowerment pushes the first level of management all the way down to those who do the work, and to some extent, every worker is then a manager. That changes the job and may often increase the market competitive pay value of the job.

The acceptance of authority by employees under empowerment and their ability to exercise that authority are critical issues that must be dealt with. Employees may need training or special support and assistance in order to work effectively when they are empowered. Some employees won't be effective in this new work environment. Restructuring jobs or staffing changes are sometimes necessary when there is a substantial change to more empowerment of workers.

Empowerment, Participation, and Involvement

There is a lot of fuzzy thinking about empowerment, and it is harmful. The words "participation" and "involvement" are bantered about as though they somehow relate to empowerment, but they are not the same.

Participation means to participate or to play a part and to make suggestions. That's far short of being empowered to make decisions.

There have been many stories about people working together and how management and employees work cooperatively and harmoniously. The stories always tell about some nice practice like participation that changed the workplace from bossism and confrontation to a place where everything was wonderful and productive. Everyone likes a good story, but not many fairy tales come true at work. Nice practices are nice, and perhaps someone should write a book about niceness at work. But the subject under consideration here is productivity, which isn't nasty or nice but is, rather, greater effectiveness and higher excellence in the workplace.

I have known many cases where stories about productivity and participation were just that. Hopefully, they were entertaining, which is probably why they were published. But they were not true and were often harmful because someone believed the story and did something stupid.

Participation is not a bad thing; it is a nice thing. Surely, participation at work is better than exclusion.

Participation is behavior at work that aims at doing certain things, such as creating an esprit de corps and making people feel like they belong. That is positive, and if that were the only choice it would be worth doing because the human gain would be worth the business cost. But participation is not the only way to make people feel like they belong and are valued. Everything that could possibly be accomplished by participation is also accomplished by empowerment. With empowerment, belonging and personal worth are accomplished without playacting.

Involvement, like participation, is not the same as empowerment. Involvement means that workers are less a part of the decision-making process than they are in participation. Involvement sometimes means only observing, listening, or being in attendance.

Employee involvement is also very nice. Involvement of any type may humanize the workplace and be an escape from boredom. Involvement has a cost, however, and this must be considered.

Involving workers in matters in which they have little to contribute will probably not do much good and might be costly. The values and the drawbacks of involvement for morale reasons are not always well understood and can have a negative impact on the workplace. Some people are likely to view unneeded involvement as pandering, and that is what it very often is.

In summary, with empowerment, workers make work decisions; with participation, workers suggest; and with involvement, employees observe. All three have a role, in some way and at some time, in employee-employer relations. In productivity management work, however, only empowerment can have an important impact on work excellence.

The Power of Empowerment

Empowerment is powerful. Empowerment can increase productivity greatly.

There are many examples of the power of empowerment. An example I often use is Schick Incorporated, partly because it is a case I experienced personally. Schick had a measured day-work production system. Expert industrial engineering consultants established the one best way for each workstation. Then there was empowerment. The employees were empowered to improve on the one best system, if they could, without compromising safety or interfering with the work of others.

Within two years, productivity had more than doubled because the workers had found many better ways of doing the work. The employees discovered work methods that fit their style and their particular attributes, things the industrial engineering consultant wouldn't have known about. In fact, the industrial engineering experts were wrong. There was not one best way for each job; there was one best way for each worker.

Schick was the first case of empowerment I was ever involved in, and the results were as dramatic as any case I have ever seen. This is partly because of the nature of manufacturing electric shavers but also because of the degree of delegation to the foremen and the empowerment to the workers that existed.

In most jobs, there is no one best way for everyone. Workers can usually find a better way to do a job than the experts. That is the main source of the power of empowerment.

When there is empowerment, employees do the work their way, not the company way. The employee's way is better, or there would be no reason to change the company way. But it is also human nature for a person to be more committed to making his or her way work better.

Part of the power of empowerment involves pride. People tend to have more pride in their work when they determine the work method. Pride power can be very great.

To understand the power of empowerment, it may be helpful to think of workers as agents of production, as human factories. For each of these production units, the correct methods of work have a lot to do with output and excellence. Whenever the range of output from acceptable levels to optimum levels is substantial, the proper process and method of work may affect the output of these individual producers greatly. Empowerment contributes to the best method of work for each worker and in that way contributes to higher levels of productivity.

Empowerment also works to increase effectiveness because everyone is working at it. You can continue to use all of the scientific management systems and all of the experts that are available and add the knowledge and experience of all of the workers in the operations.

All of these examples of the power of empowerment should encourage you to try it. Pick a location, or department, or one employee, and *do it*: delegate and empower. Be prepared to be amazed, and then implement delegative management and empowerment everywhere.

Here is one other thought to consider. Because of delegative management and empowerment, we are experiencing a silent revolution in the workplace. The first consequence will be greater productivity—much greater productivity. But other consequences will profoundly change the nature and conditions of work. For those who look for the deeper meaning of basic change, empowerment is deregulation in the workplace and a great leap forward into a new level of democracy at work.

Limits on Empowerment

Delegation and empowerment can never be complete. In fact, as more authority is granted in more areas of work, there will be other areas where more rigid requirements must be put in place. This is why McKinsey & Company often called this style of management "loose-tight."

There is always concern that if each worker has the latitude to determine work methods, he or she will make mistakes and do work ineffectively. Empowered executives, administrators, and professional experts can also make mistakes. Anyone can make mistakes, and part of effective management is to establish processes that ensure that the quality of management is high and that there is excellence of work with a minimum of errors.

As you delegate authority for work methods, there must be greater concern for and more centralized control of safety practices. Every manager and every employee must understand that the authority that is delegated is to determine *safe* work methods that are productive.

There must also be compliance with laws and government regulations. The authority is to act in compliance with all laws. The same is true about conformance to company policies and regulations.

Delegation and empowerment can't mean differences for the sake of differences. Under empowerment, exercising authority is only for the purpose of increasing the effectiveness of work. However, there should be no artificial limits on empowerment. For example, senior executives must commit to delegation and empowerment, even though the resulting practices may not be to their liking. As an example of what *not* to do, Ed Crutchfield, chief executive officer of the First Union Bank, had a temper tantrum when he called one of his employees and got a response from a voice machine. He flatly commanded that there would be no future use of such machines by anyone in "my" company. In a dictatorial and authoritarian work environment, such orders from the top may happen, but this is the antithesis of delegation and empowerment.

During the recession of the early 1990s, there was talk about taking back empowerment in order to increase profits. Top executives who thought that way never understood what empowerment was all about. You empower workers to increase the effectiveness of work and that contributes to greater profits.

Some also said that empowerment would be a victim of the cost cutting that many companies had to implement. But empowerment doesn't involve any expense at all, so that also reflected an incorrect understanding of empowerment.

There are information requirements that go with empowerment. Workers have authority to determine their work methods when there is empowerment, but they also have an obligation to let others know what they are doing, why they are doing it, and how it is done.

Empowerment is not a license for disruption. Workers and work units must consider the impact of what they do on the work of others. Greater productivity in one unit, offset by lower productivity in another unit, is zero productivity improvement.

There are management constraints on empowerment. As a manager, you empower or don't empower. With experience and changing circumstances, a manager gives more empowerment to some employees and may take away empowered authority from others. The manager consistently guides and monitors the exercise of authority of empowered workers.

Empowerment is not anarchy. There are budget and policy constraints on the actions of managers. However, compared to the neat and tidy environment of bureaucracy and regulated work, empowerment may look like chaos at times. Empowerment, however, doesn't have to result in chaos or anarchy. Rather, empowerment is a different style of management that is essential in an era of technology. Empowerment is also a style of managing that makes everyone a productivity manager.

As you consider these matters, you might agree that empowerment is often essential to high productivity and that it is a management style worth considering. If so, the question is then how to do it: How do you go about empowering employees?

Empowering

I have helped dozens of companies implement a management system of delegation and empowerment. Never have I seen two companies choose the exact same system for delegating or successfully use the same methods of implementing empowerment.

My recommended method for implementing empowerment is mostly to be *permissive*. Let employees do things one step at a time. Let them learn from experience that they are empowered and how much they are empowered under different circumstances. It has always proven to be a bad idea to try to impose empowerment on anyone. It's better to have the right people, the right environment for granting permission to act, and then let people assume authority for work methods in prescribed areas.

Don't try to empower workers by writing directives and guidelines. That's the centralized programmatic approach to management. Written guidelines haven't worked very well as a method of implementing empowerment. Such guidelines are always too elaborate and are necessarily general. Guidelines are not of much use in dealing with specifics in individual cases and circumstances.

Always focus first on delegative management. Remember that it is the operating managers who empower workers. To do this they must first have authority for the work methods delegated to them.

Empowerment is much easier to accomplish than delegative management. It is natural for an effective operating manager who has authority to delegate work-related actions to workers. Companies that have succeeded in delegating more authority to managers have found that most managers then automatically empower their subordinates in more ways or they quickly learn how to do this.

Be sure the managers know they are expected to empower workers and why. Make sure needed resources are available to the managers to help them do empowerment. The resources might only be advice and information.

It's easy and natural to empower, but it is difficult to do it well. Managers have to learn what can be empowered, and they must learn how to do it with different people under different circumstances. Managers will be empowering different matters to different people. So there may be questions about why there are differences and whether the manager has been making the right choices for the right reasons.

Empowerment is delegating, and we know from experience that it is not easy. It is more difficult, of course, when the authority and the expectation to empower are granted to people who are not experienced in delegating. Make sure the managers know the company's policy on empowerment. Make sure they know that it is their job to empower and that the success of their employees in doing empowered work will be one measure of the effectiveness of the manager.

It is always better to do something than to talk about doing it. But all employees should also know the company's policy on empowerment. Some direct communication to employees about the company's expectation regarding empowerment is usually helpful. That communication can state only intent, not specifics. However, the direct communication about the company's intent to empower puts pressure on the managers to do it.

Employees may also need guidance and support when they are empowered. These come from their direct manager. Consider some method of networking managers' experiences in empowerment so they learn from each other. Empowerment is relatively new for all of us, and we must learn from each other how to do it well.

Some think that empowerment should include self-directed work. Empowerment means latitude to determine some work matters, and by definition that is self-directed work. But there must still be manager overview to determine what is to be permitted and to provide direction in areas where there is no empowerment or where the empowerment is limited.

The idea that self-directed should mean groups of employees engaged in self-management is theoretical and experimental at best. Management is not so simple that it can be left with amateurs or conducted on the basis of a popular vote.

There have been many attempts at self-directed work over the years. These experiences have taught us that when self-directed work essentially means empowerment, there is a great potential for improved work. When self-directed work includes the work of groups of people who are supposed to manage themselves, the self-directed work has always failed. Self-directed work groups can't self-manage.

Empowered employees, like managers who have been delegated more authority, must recognize that there are practical limitations on the work they may do. With empowerment, the authority is mostly for work methods and practices. Even in these areas, however, there are limitations on authority. For example, the work must be done within safety guidelines.

Some companies have established training programs in empowerment for operating managers. These programs are crude because they are new, and the people who develop the training programs don't know much about empowerment. But even simple training sessions that do little more than discuss empowerment can help to implement empowerment.

Training in empowerment will get better, and new techniques for implementing empowerment will likely emerge. I think, however, that management activities like empowerment are always more of an art than a science and that only selection in the first place and experience in managing make people really skillful at empowerment.

Employees can learn from each other's experiences at work when there is empowerment. Some method of communicating success cases in worker-instituted work methods and some system of networking experiences with other employees would be very helpful, no matter how informal these things may be. Employees must believe that success in increasing the effectiveness of work will be rewarded. I have never seen a successful productivity pay system yet, but I have seen the same result with intelligent and well-designed salary increase plans, incentive bonus plans, and success sharing.

I have practiced as well as preached empowerment in the three different companies I headed. I had my share of success and my share of failure. In the success cases, the empowered people were always clear about what the organization was trying to accomplish.

I also learned that to empower people without controls and monitoring was a huge mistake. It is a mistake at any level of the organization, not just with lower paid workers. That's why empowerment must be from a manager to that manager's direct-reports. That's why there must be a reasonable span of management and why managers must be given the time to manage.

In the past few years, a substantial number of companies have embarked on efforts to empower their employees with more authority to do their jobs. My own experiences and close observations make me think that empowerment will be very successful. In cases I know well, the increase in productivity from empowerment has been much greater than expected.

If I am correct in thinking that most efforts at empowerment will be successful and that some will be successful beyond our imagination, then you can expect that others will follow quickly as the results of this work become known. By the end of this century, it is very likely that most companies will have in some way empowered large numbers of employees with substantial authority for how they do their work.

9

Networking

Productivity action step 8 is networking. This involves using other people's knowledge in order to do your job better. If done well, networking can often increase productivity significantly.

This is the technology era, and the amount of knowledge needed at work is increasing at a very rapid rate. There are more high-technology jobs. There is more technology in many low-technology jobs. Under these circumstances, having knowledge is clearly important to the effectiveness of work. Effective networking makes one person's knowledge and experience available to others. For these reasons, networking is an action step to consider in productivity management.

Managing knowledge is a very broad subject. To get results in productivity management work, you would be well advised to target specific areas rather than taking on the whole subject. Consider improved networking as a method of higher productivity by the better use of knowledge.

Knowledge and Productivity

Reflect on the possible impact of knowledge on the productivity of jobs in your operation. The ideas in this section are intended to help you consider how the use of knowledge and networking might contribute to greater productivity.

Networking may increase productivity by expanding the information that is available. More information *may* (or may not) increase the effectiveness of work because the information is needed immediately for a job at hand or because the information contributes to greater knowledge that will be useful at some future time. In addition, greater knowledge may contribute to higher productivity by a greater understanding or more intelligence about work.

These are complex, general, and somewhat nebulous concepts. Many businesspeople move quickly to other action steps that seem more practical. But, increasingly in this technological era, effective management involves the management of knowledge, and an important aspect of managing knowledge can be specific actions such as networking.

As noted, the management of knowledge and specific action steps can help to improve work effectiveness primarily because they expand available knowledge. This knowledge is not just information or data but may include understanding and intelligence as well. Best of all, some of the knowledge accessed in networking can be specific recommendations about how to deal with an issue.

With computers and expert systems, it may be possible to get an endless amount of facts, data, and published material. That's of value, and technology has made enormous amounts of such information available. However, it is the intelligent use of information that is most often needed to increase the effectiveness of work.

Computers make it possible to access an incredible amount of information. Theoretically, you can put all the information that has ever been printed on a computer and retrieve what you want with the push of a button. Productivity is affected by such access to information in many ways. That's why the use of technology is described as an important action step in productivity management in Chapter 6.

As discussed earlier, increasingly in knowledge work, workers must understand the information and have the know-how to use it correctly. That's partially what the management of knowledge is all about. And to the extent that a worker cannot practically possess all the knowledge needed for effective work, he or she must have access to the knowledge of others—that's network-ing.

The use of knowledge generally and networking specifically can affect the success of other action steps in productivity man-agement. Intelligence about work is key to developing useful productivity measures. Knowing which information is relevant can have a great impact on how well technology is utilized, and a knowledge of the technology is key to how well the productivity machines, such as computers, are utilized. Similarly, if you reflect on removing unproductive practices and empowerment, you may agree that knowledge and the use of information are also impor-tant in those action steps. The use of knowledge is, in fact, important in most productivity action steps.

Using knowledge to gain greater effectiveness of work in-volves:

- Getting knowledge
- Managing knowledge
- Managing knowledge workers
- Networking, including the use of experts

Getting knowledge involves more than hiring people with the knowledge needed to do the work. It also means getting people with intelligence who can learn and acquire new knowl-edge in this changing work world. Getting knowledge means hiring those with an appetite for learning and an inclination to learn. As far as networking is concerned, hiring knowledgeable people includes people with the know-how to understand what they need to know and the intelligence to ask questions and understand the answers.

The first and most important guideline for managing knowl-edge is to have an abundance of it. Basically, this means that an organization should strive to hire well-educated people at every level. Well educated means that the person is educated for the job for which he or she is hired to do *and* the work he or she is likely to be assigned in the future. At the very least, well educated means that the person is educated in the basics of English, mathematics, social science, and physical science. Well enough educated means that a person has the capacity to learn at the level at which he or she will be working and that such a person will know when to network *and* have an inclination to do so.

In networking, the management of knowledge also involves a special type of make-or-buy decision. Does each worker currently possess the knowledge required for effective work, or do the workers need to network others for what they need to know?

Managing knowledge workers involves some very special and unique skills, including time management and relating professional knowledge to the requirements of work rather than to the person's interests. Effectively managing knowledge involves good interprofessional relations so that professionals will openly share knowledge with their colleagues, in other words, so they will network. One basis for the organizational development work of the 1970s was the need for maintaining interpersonal and intergroup relationships that were good enough to have a free flow of needed knowledge between professional persons and professional groups.

Regardless of how much knowledge people have or how well knowledge workers are managed, many workers will require more information. This means networking, including the use of experts.

The Use of Experts

One key to effective networking is to use experts. If you have a problem or a question, an expert may already know what you need to find out and has the experience that will help you deal with your problem.

Here's an example of networking experts. I received a call from a client at Southland, who said he had a crisis. The company had learned that a clerk who handled food in one of its 7-Eleven stores had AIDS, and the client wanted to know what he should do.

As soon as I finished talking to him, I reflected on other clients who might know about this issue. I called Marriott, which has restaurants in all its hotels, on the theory that it might be facing this problem, too. As it turned out, Marriott had discovered months earlier that some of its kitchen workers had AIDS.

In their usual thoughtful manner, the people at Marriott examined this issue thoroughly. They networked everyone they could, including lawyers, benefit experts, physicians, and the Center for Disease Control in Atlanta. They worked out a detailed policy and procedure for dealing with this problem.

With Marriott's permission, I called Southland and outlined a recommended answer, which was essentially Marriott's answer. All of this took less than four hours of my time and was completed within a twenty-four-hour time frame. It is a wonderful example of networking and the positive effect it can have on productivity.

Don't think that you have to call a consultant to get expert information and advice. The next time you face a new question or issue, there may be people in your own company who have faced the same issue and who can provide valuable information, ideas, and suggestions.

Sometimes you need information and advice from more than one expert. I once received a call from Disney management when they were considering changing their management retirement program to a fixed benefit plan. They had been advised by an actuary to switch to a fixed benefit plan, and they wanted a second opinion. I advised them strongly not to make the change and also suggested that they get a new actuary.

Disney saved a lot of money by getting a second opinion. I spent less than two days of my time and the company's money. It is often prudent to network more than one source if the issue is important enough. If I had been called two weeks earlier, the company would have saved an additional $13 million. It also pays to network in a timely manner.

The Southland and Disney cases illustrate how using experts can save enormous amounts of time. By taking advantage of networking opportunities, productivity is much greater, the answers are better, and you often get a quicker solution.

Your organization pays experts, so why not use them? Proper networking of them can be a major source of greater productivity. You surely have accountants and lawyers and probably actuaries in your company. Most companies also hire consultants from time to time. When there is a question, ask for their input. Even an hour or so on the phone might save hundreds of hours of work.

If the problem involves just a phone call, or if the experts are being paid anyway, there should be no charge. If your question is specific, it shouldn't take more than a few hours, and that would be worth paying for if the input was good and if it saved a lot of your time.

I encourage consultants to do more network consulting. It should be a substantial part of their work. Clients should be able to call them with a specific question and get the information they need for only a few hours of billing.

Your consultant may want to turn a question into a major project. I tell companies to act like customers and insist on network consulting, or get someone who will provide what the customer wants. The average network assignment is about five hours of billed time. The work is usually done by phone and mail and the elapsed time is very short.

One problem with using experts is that they may not be available or they may be less available to operating managers and those who work at locations, in contrast to those who work in the corporate office. This is usually because the consultants' fees are so high that they can be considered only for systemwide projects. But the need is for more networking and less new project work. On an information network basis, it may be cost-effective to use consultants for networking knowledge in the operations as well as in the home office.

At certain times and in certain ways, experts should be available to managers at every level and in every part of the organization. They must be expert in dealing with the questions encountered in the operations, and they must be accessible. Experts should also be available to operating managers in many functional areas, including the use of technology, finance, union relations, safety, legal compliance, and human resources management.

The obvious expert to network on operational matters is the manager's immediate manager. There will be times when the manager's manager can't help, and then other sources of information must be available through networking.

This is an area of great organizational need. With delegative management and empowerment, the authority to determine work methods has been pushed down in the organization. Access to information about how to do work effectively must be pushed down in the organization, too.

Staff people in areas such as finance and personnel must increasingly be more of a network for the knowledge needed by operations managers at every level. These staff experts should be spending less time explaining and enforcing fewer programs and relatively more time providing advice and useful knowledge to the managers.

The greater challenge is to make the operational experts available to the operating managers in addition to the higher level managers throughout the company. Few experts are available on operating issues. Most are not likely to do network consulting because they can make much more money doing project work.

But the user is the customer, and the client companies are insisting more and more that their consultants are available for networking. The operating knowledge is often the critical thing that must be possessed or accessed by the organization. Customers of consultants must insist on networking as one of the services.

Worknetworking

Networking involves receiving needed information and transmitting information or knowledge others need for their work. Thus networking involves exchanging information and knowledge. For this reason, I often call it "worknetworking."

Knowledge Needs

Managers, professionals, and many workers could read literature nonstop and listen to tapes all day and still not know everything needed to do an effective job. Regardless of how experienced and smart these people might be, they need access to knowledge they don't have personally, at least from time to time, in order to work effectively. Information needs in an increasing number of jobs are greater than the time available to learn. There is continuous change, so there is always more to learn. Some of what we already know is no longer correct or relevant and must be purged, which is a special form of learning.

As we try to learn as much as we reasonably can to keep abreast of information needed at work, we are subject to a continuous stream of unfiltered information from random sources, authored by variously qualified persons. These sources provide information in an indiscriminate manner. They tell you what you already know, what you need to know, and what you don't need to know in unpredictable mixes. And with these sources, you generally have to start at page one and read everything to get the few parts you really need.

Many meetings and conferences are designed for networking. Obviously, the knowledgeability of the meeting leader is critical, but it is more than that. Meetings and conferences have agendas that reflect mostly what the speaker knows, or what the speaker thinks you should know. The speaker doesn't know what you need to know, and rarely are you asked what you *think* you need to know.

Authors and speakers have various credentials, and there is often little correlation between the expertise of the writer or speaker and his or her prominence. In fact, it is increasingly novelists and entertainers who get the most media attention with respect to all communications, including business information.

Networking for Knowledge Needs

There is thus a great need for quality information and a capacity to screen the information you get. That need can be dealt with automatically with effective worknetworking. If your contacts are true experts, the information accessed should be correct and relevant. If they respond to your information requests when you need them, then the information you get from worknetworking is also always relevant and timely.

You must recognize that some of those from whom you get knowledge in worknetworking will help you because they want you to be in their network and help them. Thus you also must be prepared to give information even though this takes your time.

None of us has as much information as we need or may

need. Most of us have a knowledge gap. The time we have available and our capacity for acquiring more knowledge are not likely to change, but the amount of knowledge we need is continuing to grow. Furthermore, with advances in the technology of communications, a lot more information will be available and a higher and higher percentage of it will be incorrect or not relevant.

People don't know what they'll need to know in the future. Often you find out what you don't know when you are asked a question or when you have a problem. That's when you need worknetworking the most. You then need the knowledge immediately, and you must get it from a proven source.

Knowledge Possessed

In business and in the knowledge areas of business, the intelligent manager or professional needs to be familiar with a proper sample of knowledge about the fields of work involved. Only then can either the manager or the professional function effectively. But there is then also the need to access knowledge not possessed, and the correct sample of knowledge on the part of the intelligent manager, professional, or worker is essential in order to select from among an almost endless amount of available knowledge.

We also need to have a correct sample of knowledge in our field so we know what questions to ask. Effective worknetworking depends on skills of asking as well as knowing the people to ask. For this reason, our ability to ask and listen will have to improve in this technology era.

So you need knowledge, a correct sample of knowledge. And you still need a stream of new knowledge to make sure that you are up-to-date and maintain a proper sample of knowledge of the fields in which you work. You have to be knowledgeable when you access information because you must be able to evaluate what you get. However, the evaluation job is simplified enormously if you have a good network of trusted and reliable people.

Don't assume that you can get additional information by traditional learning methods. No one always has the time to accumulate all the information required, evaluate it, and then come to a conclusion. Furthermore, there is sometimes a need for quick reaction, and there isn't the time to go through the traditional problem-solving and decision-making approaches.

Knowledge Networked

Part of the answer to effective networking must be to set up your own worknetworking system. The type of knowledge required will include mostly the following:

- Facts, data, historical events, or other information that someone else has readily available but would take a lot of time to get on your own.
- Information about experiences, good or bad, in some areas where you have no experience, or where your experience is limited.
- Identifying available alternatives, perhaps just a scan of the most likely possibilities.
- Questions about a specific case or incident.
- Questions about legal, accounting, or other technical consequences of actions you are considering.
- Opinions or commentary, usually about a controversial matter.

In worknetworking, the more specific the question or request, the more specific the response is likely to be. It is the very specific responses that make worknetworking the most useful. For example, ask an expert for a briefing on jobs training, and it will take about one week of the expert's time and your money, and a total time of about a month. The response would necessarily be very general. Ask about retraining tool-and-die makers made surplus by CAD for jobs elsewhere in your organization and that will take a day of the expert's time, with rather specific answers in two or three days. Ask about others who have had this problem and the response will be very specific, with an hour or two of the expert's time and your answer arriving probably within twenty-four hours.

Establishing Networks

We all have worknetworks now. Therefore, each person in each organizational unit should start to build the networks needed by evaluating those that exist. Many of the contacts you now use are part of the organizational structure of your company, and you can't change that. Start by learning to network the organizational structure in which you work.

Examine carefully all your other worknetwork arrangements. Many of them were acquired by chance. Evaluate carefully the value and the time cost of your existing relationships. If existing worknetworks don't meet all of your needs for knowledge, build new ones consciously and carefully. Build your worknetworks a step at a time, over a period of time.

To be productive in your work, you should consider a number of worknetworks. Establish each carefully.

The first focus should always be on establishing an effective worknetwork in your own company. Be sure you have access to the best knowledge available in your organization for dealing with company problems and issues.

Consider worknetworks with respected people in similar companies. You should include only those who have something of value to contribute and who want to be a part of such a working relationship. Depending upon the level of your job and the nature of your work, you might also consider a "leader group." This would include people thought to be very knowledgeable in areas where you likely need information from time to time.

Establishing a network is a project. It will take a personal time investment to build a good worknetwork, but it is worth it. Setting up such worknetworks may be one of the most important single actions you undertake in your career.

Depending on the type of work you do, worknetworking can be extremely important to work effectiveness. To illustrate, I use my own experience.

I left Sibson & Company in 1977, taking about fifty clients with me. I had no staff in Vero Beach. People asked how I could keep abreast of the field without a staff or consulting associates. The answer was that I have a large worknetwork. It includes the staff people in client companies. In addition, I have a list of about three dozen people, each of whom I regard as an expert in some area of human resources management. I often refer to these people as The Sibson Group, but there is no organization. They are just people I network and who network me.

I need a large network in my work. A first-level operating manager would need only a few people in his or her network in addition to the next higher level manager and the company's own staff.

Worknetworks are the new organizations of this decade. They exist at every level and in every area of an organization. I think worknetworking will be a big thing in the twenty-first century. For many people, it will be a big boost in productivity. For some, their networks may be the key to personal success.

Using Worknetworking

The value of networks is in using them, not just in setting them up. Sometimes people are much better at the setting-up process. There is a natural disinclination to ask questions or ask for help, and this is a big problem in the use of networks. It's not so much that people fear asking a dumb question as it is a concern about being thought of as being ignorant.

In the knowledge era, success will often go to those who ask. I put high on the list of communications skills the skill of asking and the skill of listening. Some will say that they don't have the time to ask questions. These are the people with weakness in the skill of asking.

Unlike attorneys, businesspeople generally only ask a question if they don't know the answer. And the smart businessperson always seeks the best answer in the shortest time. Therefore, asking in worknetworking is designed to save time, not expend it.

Some will say that their boss expects them to know it all. Unfortunately, there are bosses like that. However, the intelligent manager wants people who are knowledgeable but smart enough to realize what they don't know and who are prudent enough to ask.

Knowledge is a business resource. Like any business resource, it must be used judiciously and in a cost-efficient manner. Your organization's knowledge resource includes the knowledge of your people and the knowledge they can access. A higher percentage of this organizational know-how resource is accessed and must be networked. This is an important and subtle form of outsourcing.

The cost of knowledge resources is mostly a time cost rather than an equipment cost. These time costs are mainly your own payroll expenses. The amount of consulting fees for networking is negligible, and that's particularly true of consulting costs based on accessing know-how from consultants rather than using them for projects.

It is important to note that networking is essentially at the discretion of each worker. It is delegated authority and empowerment. Organizational systems like budgeting plus high-level management may restrict or guide networking, but networking is essentially done or not done by operating managers and empowered workers.

To Keep in Mind

The first four of the twelve required action steps are basically driven from the top, but the next four, including networking, are discretionary and are basically driven by operating managers throughout the company. These are also the action steps that an operating manager can do regardless of what the corporation does.

Even if you work for a company that doesn't care about productivity, you could still do the following:

* Utilize computer technology to increase productivity.
* Remove unproductive practices in your operation.
* Empower your employees—at least somewhat more.
* Develop information networks.

No manager was ever fired or disciplined for doing these things. And if the results are better, the manager is praised. But praise or not, if a manager can take such actions and improve the excellence of work at his or her own initiative with existing resources, the manager should do it.

The last four productivity action steps, 9 through 12, are driven by human resources professionals, or at least they depend upon the excellence of personnel work. Each of the last four recommended steps is covered in the following four chapters. They are dependent upon human resources practices, namely, staffing, organizational structuring, performance management, and reward for performance.

10

Using an Employment Strategy to Increase Productivity

If your organization is staffed by highly productive and self-motivated people, you will have high levels of productivity. Staffing an organization, step 9, is an important step in productivity management.

There is an old saying in personnel work, "Put your personnel dollars up front." This action step in the EP process applies that principle to productivity management. Hire more productive people and you will have a more productive workforce.

Staffing can be one of the most important single practices for increasing productivity. In many companies, productivity can be improved a full 10 percent by better staffing. Furthermore, recruiting better workers is a strategic action that can have an ongoing favorable impact on productivity. In addition, it is generally true that it is easier to improve productivity by better employment practices than by training.

An Employment Strategy for Productivity Improvement

The employment strategy for increasing productivity is very simple. Hire better people; hire more effective workers. Hire more effective workers than those you have now. Hire workers who are more effective than those who work in competitive organizations. More effective means those whose performance is better; those whose output is greater. More effective workers mean more productive workers and nothing else.

The formula for improving productivity through the use of an employment strategy requires that you hire people with more talent, the highest level of honesty, and great ambition. Specifically, talent, ambition, and honesty mean the following:

- *Talent* is a natural ability or aptitude for work and a capacity for achievement.
- *Ambition* is an earnest desire for achievement or distinction and a willingness to strive for it.
- *Honesty* is the quality of always being truthful, having integrity, and a predictable commitment to one's obligations and contracts, formal or otherwise.

These are the qualities you should seek in every worker you recruit. As you succeed in recruiting more people with greater talent, ambition, and honesty, you will get a more productive workforce. Recruiting better people is difficult and requires talent, effort, and time. The basic attributes you should seek to improve productivity are difficult to evaluate.

Honesty is the most difficult human success quality to evaluate. It is easy to sort out people who lie, but the tough cases are people who tell the truth in such a way that you don't hear the truth. The quality you seek with respect to honesty includes integrity and dependability.

Everyone has some ambition, at least the ambition to survive. The scarce quality is the willingness to strive for achievement. Look for those who always do their reasonable best in work, in play, or in anything else.

Everyone except the most disadvantaged person has some talent. Search for those with distinctly better than average talent in areas where you need it. Look particularly for those who have a talent and an appetite for learning and who adapt well to change. Among these people, look for those who have an inclination to apply what they have learned to the needs of an organization.

Of the three success attributes, honesty and ambition should be "go" or "no-go" qualities. For example, a person must be honest or should be screened out. If a person is "sort of" honest, or "sometimes" honest, or "not really" dishonest, that person is not honest and should be eliminated from consideration for employment. To have high productivity, an organization needs people who are "just plain" honest.

People must have ambition or they must be screened out and eliminated in the employment process. There is a minimum amount of ambition that every employee must have in a successful enterprise. This basic level must be sufficient to reflect an effectiveness ethic. In addition, each person must be inclined to do his or her reasonable best at work.

Talent is the great variable, and at any level of work, the range from the least talented to the most talented can be very wide. Even in low-technology, nonskilled jobs, the output of the most talented person (who is honest and ambitious) is usually at least a third more than the least talented person (who is also honest and ambitious). In knowledge jobs, the difference in output between the most talented and least talented can be 1,000 percent.

Of course, everyone must be qualified to do the job they are hired to perform. When this employment strategy is implemented, the most talented person from among those qualified is hired, not necessarily the person who is best qualified to do the job that is being filled. This is strategic hiring, because it aims for building talent for the long term rather than just getting people up to speed in the job being filled in the shortest amount of time.

There have been well-known cases where companies set out to get better people and were successful. They reported their efforts and their successes. IBM has long been known as always hiring the "IBM type." The company surely went after talent, ambition, and honesty with great energy and lush employment terms. The success of IBM was thought to be due largely to the great talent of the people who worked for the company. But IBM also considered appearance and manners when selecting people and particularly their willingness to go along and do things the

Big Blue way. Those characteristics may have caused some of the company's recent problems. In any event, with a new IBM there should be a rethinking of strategic recruiting requirements.

Bell Labs has said publicly that a large part of its success in invention is recruiting the top professionals. The process evaluates candidates against the technical people the company has and the technical people the competition has. Bell Labs wants the best and consistently looks for better professionals. This case also has a side interest in that when AT&T was spun off and faced the real world of competition, Bell Labs' specifications had to be modified to take into consideration even more the inclination of people to focus on the practical needs of their customers.

GE publicly reported that it recruited twice as many people as it needed for management programs. GE tried to recruit the best and then kept only the most successful half from among these. GE does a lot less of this now because it found the process was very costly and that it was training competitors.

Three things are common to all employment strategy cases, including the three described above. First, the strategy is rarely applied to all jobs, but rather focuses on the strategically most important jobs. Second, the selection criteria must be changed as the company's business circumstances change. Third, in all cases, the purpose was to attain high levels of productivity, and there has been remarkable success in many of the employment strategy cases in increasing employee productivity.

Any company can apply this productivity action step. Any organizational unit within a company can also apply it. Consider this productivity action step for at least some jobs.

Labor Markets, Talent Scarcity, and This Employment Strategy

As the economy moves more and more into the technology era, capabilities that exist in labor markets are becoming more disparate. The knowledge differences are greater, skill levels are greater, and the performance spread between best and marginal performers is much greater than before. Furthermore, labor markets have become more and more fissionable, in the sense that there are more types of jobs and more specialties within fields of work. It is these characteristics that make possible the use of this employment strategy to improve productivity.

Don't underestimate these changes in labor markets or their impact on recruitment and employment. A few simple illustrations might help to point out the growing differences in labor markets and the impact on recruiting. Companies should make specific analyses for their own jobs and in their own labor markets.

Take as one example the education and learning capabilities of those in the workforce. The gap between the well educated and the also graduated has been growing dramatically for thirty years. In public education, the quality of top-ranked graduates has been improving steadily by small amounts while the level of the also graduated has declined shockingly. That trend is continuing, and the spread between the top graduates and the also graduated continues to become greater.

Social forces have similarly changed the work attitudes and inclinations of those in the workforce. The striving for excellence by some is as great as ever. For an equal number of people, the effectiveness ethic does not exist. In my opinion, whole classes and categories of people in the labor market have been led to believe that they are entitled. They believe they are entitled to jobs and higher pay because of their category, and that qualifications for work, effort, or performance should not count.

Many workers in special categories have been encouraged to think that they can be successful regardless of honesty, ambition, and talent. They have been encouraged to think they are entitled by the leaders of their special interest groups who preach entitlement and by the employers who lure them into their workplaces by giving preferential treatment of various sorts in order to meet quotas of one type or another.

Another example of the opportunity for greater productivity through better staffing relates to significant talent shortages in labor markets. There are not enough well-educated people to go around, and in some fields, such as computers, electronics, genetics, and robotics, there are shortages of skills and experience as well as deficiencies in education.

It is difficult to estimate the magnitude of the chronic talent shortage partly because jobs are filled with less than fully qualified people. My guess is that there are more jobs unfilled or inadequately filled than there are unemployed persons, even during a recession, and that talent shortages probably number 15 million.

This is the most important aspect of the jobs issue in this country. Of course, we would like low unemployment, but in a rapidly changing economy, 5 or 6 percent unemployment is an absolute minimum percentage of unemployed or between employment. An unemployment rate of 7 percent needs to be worked on, but only to get it down to the minimum level of 5 or 6 percent.

When it comes to unfilled or underfilled jobs, it is necessary for the index to be near zero. We can't compete in international markets with more than 7 percent of all jobs filled to meet quotas or on the basis that it is better to have a poorly qualified person fill a job than to have no one at all. The real jobs issue is to get better educated and trained workers who are qualified for every job.

These are the principal conclusions from a study of labor market characteristics that related to the use of an employment strategy to increase the effectiveness of work. It would be very useful to do more research on the subject, and I believe we know how the work should be done.

The conclusions of this work are important, and they suggest three things:

1. There are enormous differences in the talent of those who might be recruited.
2. Whereas there is a serious shortage of talent in the economy overall, plenty of talent is available for any single company, regardless of how large that employer might be.
3. The adoption of a strategy to increase productivity by applying an employment strategy has worked before and will work today.

Organizational Enrichment

The employment strategy can be used to fill open jobs or to replace current employees. If a company does replace some of its current workers with more effective workers from outside, it is engaging in "organizational enrichment."

Organizational enrichment means outplacing current workers who are poor or marginal performers and replacing them with high performers recruited from the labor market. With organizational enrichment, you create turnover among low performers and replace them with high performers. Organizational enrichment often involves promotions. The job of the person outplaced is filled from within by promoting a better performer. Then a more productive person is recruited to fill the job of the person who is outplaced. One outplacement can mean three or four promotions for high performers. Then even mature companies with stable overall employment can have high growth for high performers.

In fact, for some time in some companies, it may be more practical to increase productivity through organizational enrichment than through training and development. The ability of a company to increase people's effectiveness and to change them is very often less than the company's ability to recruit.

A well-known company recently undertook a formal system of organizational enrichment. Using a special performance appraisal system, this company identified performers in the bottom 5 percent. These employees were then targeted for outplacement and were replaced by more effective people. The actual job openings were filled mostly by promotion from within, and ultimately the company recruited more effective employees. It took five rounds of organizational enrichment before this company reached the point where the replacement candidates were not clearly more capable than those identified for outplacement.

Organizational enrichment is harsh medicine. It involves some very sensitive issues. To make it work, your company needs a high level of excellence in certain areas, for example, recruiting. There must also be reliable systems of performance appraisal.

There must be systems and people who will focus only on performance and capability in this work.

You must also consider the cost of organizational enrichment, which can be substantial. When a company takes on this approach, it should make a special effort at first helping the marginal performers to improve. The volume of job changes in organizational enrichment is also the cause of a significant cost of disruption. The prudent company that does organizational enrichment would also establish very careful discrimination reviews. Whatever it does, the company must recognize that its actions invite compliance cases.

In organizational enrichment, you don't have to be successful every time. In fact, you may even have some organizational downgrading, or the ultimate replacements may be less talented than the people who were outplaced. Productivity will be significantly increased if your organizational enrichment program results in more talent in three of ten cases, even if the result is downgrading in one of ten cases.

If you consider this action, be sure that it is fairly and effectively managed. With respect to current employees, be certain that the organization makes a commitment to employee success. Before considering outplacement and replacement, make sure that the company has done what it should to improve the performance of marginal workers. Make very sure that the basis of determining people for outplacement is really performance and not bias. Then be very certain that the people recruited are clearly better performers, better enough to pay the cost of the enrichment.

Implementation

Any version of an employment strategy to increase productivity requires that the organization has excellence in recruitment and selection. If you can't be assured that you will pick candidates with higher talent, this is not a strategy for your company. At any point in time, any company can significantly improve the excellence of its employment. Almost always, even relatively easy and low-cost action steps can increase employment excellence measurably.

The difference in time or cost between recruiting and selection practices that are good enough and those that are truly excellent is often rather modest, yet the results can be enormous. So the economics of better recruiting are very positive.

The impact of recruiting better talent on results is clear and dramatic in sports and entertainment. I think that the effect of talent on organizational results is just as great, even though the link is not always clear in business.

When I was conducting conferences, I gave a lecture series on human talent and enterprise success. In one lecture, I started with the following statement:

> If you want to start a business, there is one certain approach that will ensure success. Find a small number of highly talented people, each of whom is basically honest and all of whom are very ambitious. You don't need a large number of people; less than ten will do. Among your group, be sure there are some knowledge and experience in the basics of business: marketing, production, and finance. Be very certain that each person in your group is skilled in the management of people. You don't need any money; you don't even need a business idea. You just need talent. Your business will make money by the end of the first year, and within five years, you can sell out to some big corporation, and the original group of ten or less will all be multimillionaires.

I think that this idea is just as valid for existing organizations as it is in starting a business. Better people will get better results. That's the essence of this action step in productivity management.

You could argue that if everyone did recruiting with excellence you couldn't get better people, which would be theoretically correct. But not all organizations recruit with excellence. Many companies do good recruiting, but for others, recruiting is randomly good at best. Some companies actually set out to get poor performers, or at least their recruiting system is designed to do so. In such an environment, it is easy to implement a strategy for increasing productivity through better employment.

Start by picking a department or a particular family of jobs. Take the action steps described in this chapter with respect to these jobs. Measure results carefully and keep track of the extra recruiting costs, if there are any. As long as the value is clearly greater than the incremental cost, keep going.

You will probably get resistance to implementing this action step. Sometimes there is resistance to the notion of better recruiting because of ignorance of opportunities or lack of confidence in the ability of the recruiters. Most often, resistance to recruiting better people is based on fairness questions. But there can't be any serious objections to recruiting better workers. The objections are always that some person involved in the employment process will be biased or that recruiting better people will not give preferential treatment to some group.

From the start, I urge companies to track two pieces of data very carefully. Check the performance spread of the people who are newly recruited over those formerly employed and keep careful track of the cost. Make sure that you also keep track of any change in the mix of the workforce. Changes in the demographic mix of the workforce, particularly minorities, females, and disabled persons, must be monitored carefully because you know that it will be a potential issue.

Sometimes the best actions are the simplest ones. Improving productivity by recruiting more productive people is a very simple and direct plan, and it works.

11

Restructuring

Another commonsense method of increasing employee productivity is by restructuring. As productivity action step 10, restructuring refers to actions an organization takes to change its work structure or its work focus in order to improve work excellence.

In recent years, restructuring by some of the best-known companies has received a lot of attention from the media because it resulted in large cutbacks in employment. For many other companies, restructuring has had a less dramatic but substantial impact on productivity. Restructuring actions must be customized to each organization. Mostly, however, restructuring has meant streamlining the organizational structure, reducing staff and support activities, using more contract workers, and refocusing the business.

Organizational Streamlining

There has been a great deal of organizational restructuring in American business during the past ten years. There is likely to be just as much in the next ten years. A great deal of this work has been organizational streamlining, which mostly means eliminating at least one organizational level. For example, if there are eight organizational levels from the chief executive officer to the nonsupervisory workers, at least one of those levels is eliminated.

Levels are usually removed one at a time. Rarely is one level removed uniformly throughout the organization. Instead, one organizational level is removed from many units, there is no streamlining in some, and others are streamlined a lot.

Business Practices

In 1992 I conducted a survey that covered many aspects of organizational structuring and included a number of questions on the subject. More than 300 companies, each with more than 200 employees, participated in this study. One-fourth of all the companies had conducted organizational streamlining within the past three years. That is big news, and yet organizational streamlining has rarely been reported in the journals of business and never as front-page news, except in cases involving large-scale layoffs.

That same survey showed that more than half of the participating companies planned to streamline their organizations even more within the next few years. Almost half were planning their second or third such effort.

There is a great opportunity for considerable organizational streamlining in many operations because so many levels were added, a step at a time, in the forty years following World War II. Based on a number of studies, businesses with more than 500 employees increased the number of organizational levels from an average of about seven in 1950 to an average of more than ten by 1990. Because of organizational streamlining, the average number of levels in companies with 500 or more employees is now down to somewhat less than nine. I predict that by the year 2000 the number of organizational levels in larger companies will be down to seven, which is what they were back in 1950.

Growth of Hierarchal Organizations—1950 to 1990

There are many reasons why organizational levels increased during the forty-year period from 1950 to 1990. It is helpful to understand why organizations grew more hierarchal as one input to determining actions to streamline. Here are the principal factors that led to a 50 percent increase in the number of organizational levels during that period:

1. Government regulations required a lot more work. Much of this work was highly specialized and led to the establishment of many special technical areas. One consequence was more organizational levels to provide supervision.
2. This was the period of scientific management, and many programs and regulations were established. It was the era of bureaucratic and centralized management, and the number of organizational levels seemed unimportant.
3. There were recognition reasons to add organizational levels. Job evaluation plans, for example, rewarded people for more organizational levels as well as more employees. A person was often "promoted" to a higher level in the organization as a way of recognition.
4. The model or reference for management practices during this period was mostly very large, unionized, smokestack businesses. Centralized and highly structured hierarchal organizations seemed to work in these companies at that time, and many organizational levels seemed to be a necessary part of business.
5. Formal and hierarchal styles of management were taught in business schools and written about by the organizational gurus.
6. Some companies genuinely thought that some of the added organization was a business-building investment for the future.
7. Many new organizational activities emerged, such as personnel. It seemed necessary to break down the organization into discrete pieces for each of these activities, but many of these pieces were small. This also led to more organizational levels, partly because these small units had to be managed.
8. Many of the bellwether companies could afford fat organizations, so there were few restrictions on spending for more people and more elaborate organizations.
9. Organizational theory was a fad during some of these years. Consultants did a lot of work in structuring and, predictably, they invented complicated organizations that were more and more hierarchal. A lot of "principles"

for structuring emerged and became part of the culture of business, and many of these rules and principles encouraged more and more layers of organization.

10. This was the era of focus on interpersonal relations, and that seemed to require separate identity and status for more and more special working groups, which also added to the number of organizational levels.

Identifying some of the factors that caused an increase in the number of organizational levels provides clues to how to reduce them. For example, reward good work with pay and promotion rather than with organizational status.

Need for Organizational Streamlining

Clearly, business can no longer afford hierarchal organizations. International competitive pressures and other economic conditions of the 1990s require leaner and quicker companies.

The driving forces behind organizational streamlining today are twofold. Streamlining reduces payroll and broadens the span of management (see Chapter 4). Organizational streamlining means fewer people. Eliminate one organizational level and you eliminate a lot of people. Generally speaking, the elimination of just one such level results in a reduction in employment of more than 10 percent.

In addition to reducing payroll, organizational streamlining contributes to greater productivity in a number of ways. Most important, a flatter organization means a broader span of management. This means a higher ratio of supervised persons to managers, and as noted earlier, this makes the time spent on managing more productive.

A broader span of management also makes bigger management jobs. This can mean fewer but better managers.

A flatter organization improves communications. One less organizational level means one less organizational obstacle to effective communications.

In streamlined organizations, there tends to be quicker reaction to issues, and quicker reaction in a work world characterized by more change and more rapid change is important to effectiveness. Streamlined organizations can react quicker because the decision makers are closer to the activities that require action.

Streamlining

Based mostly on the experiences of the 1980s and the 1990s, here are guidelines for the number of organizational levels a company should have, counting the chief executive officer as one organizational level and nonsupervisory workers as another:

- Very large companies (usually more than 50,000 employees): seven to nine levels.
- Large companies (generally with more than 5,000 but fewer than 50,000 employees): five to seven levels.
- Intermediate-size companies (more than 500 but fewer than 5,000 employees): four or five levels.
- Moderate-size companies (more than 100 but fewer than 500 employees): three or four levels.
- Small companies (more than ten but fewer than 100 employees): two or three levels.
- Very small companies (fewer than ten employees): two levels.

Organizational streamlining is a difficult undertaking that requires a deep knowledge of the operations. When jobs are eliminated in any manner, including streamlining, work is eliminated. In organizational streamlining, the goal is to streamline work, not just eliminate jobs. Needed work in jobs eliminated must be reassigned to other jobs that remain.

When there is restructuring there is a regrouping of work, and generally there are broader groupings. As an example, this might result in all types of plant engineering work being in one unit, which is directed by one manager who would have a different discipline background than many of the people in the combined department.

Regrouping is complicated. It results in new work clusters and new work relationships, often means merging disciplines, and represents a dramatic change. The competence required in organizational streamlining is a knowledge of the operations and an understanding of the technical aspects of the work being done.

Because of the requirements, it has always been my view that operating managers rather than staff organizational experts or consultants should spearhead organizational streamlining. Obviously, the managers must be at a substantially higher level in the organization than the jobs being streamlined. These managers must have authority that spans all the units likely to be regrouped and cannot personally be directly affected by the streamlining.

I also suggest a bottom-up approach. I urge companies to start the streamlining process at the first or lowest organizational level. Most organizations are not as hierarchal at the first levels of management, so this is the easiest place to begin. There are also fewer organizational sacred cows in the lower organizational levels and, therefore, there is less opposition to change.

The Producers

In addition to organizational streamlining, many companies have been restructuring by eliminating staff and support positions. This is another opportunity for increasing employee productivity.

Just as American businesses generally added organizational levels in the decades from 1950 to 1990, they also added staff and support positions. The bureaucratic and administrative methods of the time required many staff people. For example, staff experts were needed to design and implement all of the programs adopted during this era of scientific management practices. In the field I know best, which is personnel, the staff organization grew enormously for forty years. From a personnel ratio of about 0.6 percent in 1950, ratios grew to more than 1.2 percent by 1990. Now those personnel ratios are headed down. The organizational survey noted earlier indicated that personnel ratios were now averaging somewhat less than 1.0. By the turn of the century, the personnel ratios in all American businesses will probably be at about 0.6 percent again.

In 1960, very few companies had a corporate personnel organization. Almost all of personnel organizations were at the locations, and they supported operating management directly.

That's why I mostly did my personnel consulting directly for the chief executive officer. There were few corporate personnel officers or high-level corporate personnel functional specialists.

Over the years, I urged many companies to add someone at the corporate office to administer the programs I was hired to develop and implement. What started with one or a few people became a cast of many, with fancy titles and big pay checks. But restructuring is changing all of that.

Don't think that overstaffing occurred only in personnel. It happened in every part of the operation. Usually financial departments expanded the most in terms of number of people, and legal departments had the most bloated payrolls. All of this is also changing.

For whatever reason, American companies simply became overstaffed. Generally speaking, the larger the organization, the more it was overweighed with staff and support people at the corporate office. American management isn't lazy and it isn't dumb, but it *is* fat. One restructuring activity is to peal off the layers of fat that have grown over the past forty years.

When reviewing this issue, think about four types of work that is done in every organization. These four types of work and four types of workers are:

- *Producing work*. People who are actually producing or selling a product or service.
- *Support work*. Workers who are doing things that are necessary for the producers to do their work. This would include research and development, maintaining machines, schedulers, and such.
- *Managing work*. People who are really managing, spending a majority of their time on hiring, assigning work, training, and the like.
- *Other*. This includes all other work.

At the end of World War II, 80 percent of all the people in this country were doing producing work. About 5 percent of employees were doing managing work, 5 percent were doing support work, and 10 percent were doing other work. Today, fewer than half of all workers are doing producing work. The proportion of managers has doubled. "Other" workers have increased fivefold. We are working hard, but we aren't producing enough. We need to have more people working hard at producing quality products and services.

In companies with fewer than 100 employees, 80 percent of all workers are producers. The company that has more than 100 employees can also have 80 percent of its employees doing producing work. That should be the goal of all companies. It would do a lot to rightsize the American workforce and increase employee productivity.

I first got the idea of emphasizing producing work and those workers who are doing producing work from John Park, who was the chief executive officer of American Stores, with whom I worked for many years. John would always insist that the focus be on helping store managers and others who were doing producing work to be more effective in their jobs. There were few staff and support jobs at the corporate level at American Stores, and it was very clear that they were to help the producers work more effectively.

Many of those who hear my presentations on the EP process of productivity management or read this book will not be producers. I am not a producer by my own definition. So there is no suggestion that we nonproducers are of no value. Rather, there have been far too many of us. Organizations are very overstaffed, and an important part of restructuring is to reduce the staff, support, and management workers and therefore increase the proportion of the workforce that are producers.

Downsizing

Organizational streamlining and cutbacks in staff jobs have resulted in massive downsizing. Downsizing has been big news. It means having fewer people for a given level of activity or volume of sales. It means fewer hours of work for a volume of activity. It means higher productivity.

Downsizing results in layoffs. Much downsizing has been from the substitution of equipment for human effort. A great deal has also come from restructuring and a reduction in staff and support positions.

Don't underestimate the degree to which downsizing has occurred in some sections of some companies. I made a presentation in 1989 to the fourteen corporate personnel department heads at Ryder in Miami. Today, there is no corporate personnel staff at all.

Every organization should consider downsizing. A 5 percent productivity gain from downsizing is a realistic target for many organizations. Here are some thoughts to consider if you decide to downsize:

- Reassigning corporate staff, support, and service jobs into the operations helps downsizing. When these jobs are reassigned into the operation, their activities become more user-responsive.
- Identify activities that are clearly necessary to meet the legal, accounting, or fiduciary responsibilities of the corporation and those that are necessary to reasonably manage the risks. All other staff and support jobs should be contributive in nature. Examine each of these by a zero-based activity value analysis method.
- Getting rid of obsolete business practices throughout the company can eliminate many jobs.
- Recognize that downsizing, like reduction in force, cannot be accomplished simply by eliminating jobs and reducing the number of people. Ultimately, the task must be to eliminate work or to increase work effectiveness.
- Look for opportunities to eliminate an activity completely. Certain types of inspection operations, for example, may be eliminated if the work is done correctly the first time.
- Be as certain as possible that work is eliminated and not postponed. Downsizing follows upsizing, and future upsizing may follow some of today's downsizing.
- Delegate the job of downsizing to departments and people who are to be downsized. Set downsizing targets, but let those who are close to the operation eliminate levels and cut out jobs.

- You should not have to hire consultants for this work, except perhaps for information and briefings.

Downsizing is generally regarded as a major project, because this is what has happened so often in the 1990s. Actually, downsizing is best done in small bites, having time to look directly at the work to be eliminated rather than at the bodies to be removed.

Refocusing

A lot of the organizational structuring involves streamlining, but there also has been work on structuring the company to meet customers' needs better and on emphasizing the quality of work.

As one example of restructuring for closer customer responsiveness, some companies are organizing into businesses based on common customers. In other companies, there is less direction from marketing executives at the top and more authority for marketing with those who have contact with customers. That authority for marketing goes with everyone who has customer contact and is also reflected in organizational structuring.

Most of what has been described as organizational refocusing has not involved any change in the structure. Often, refocusing changes few practices. What is changed is the style of managing, employee attitudes, or both.

Refocusing generally involves a major communications effort to get companies to look outward relatively more and inward relatively less. Refocusing is said to be toward customers, to their needs and requirements. If nothing else, refocusing attempts to have everyone be far more concerned about the quality and reliability of the company's products and services.

In a sense, refocusing involves measures designed to get more of an effectiveness ethic. The massive effort involves not only conversations but extreme efforts of all types to get workers' attention focused on the importance of an effectiveness ethic and on methods of meeting the customers' requirements.

Of course, many jobs in an organization don't have an effect on its customers, except cost and correctness of work. But a constant emphasis on quality and a constant striving to serve the customer better are thought by some to get workers to be more effective in their work.

With refocusing, there is often relatively less reliance on testing and centralized quality checks and relatively more emphasis on building in quality up front and having people do the work correctly the first time. Doing work correctly the first time is certainly not a new idea, but it is heavily employed in refocusing, partly to correct the poor quality of work in the past.

A lot of productivity efforts under some highly publicized methods seem to rely heavily on massive efforts and constant communications to get employees to do their jobs as they are supposed to. In the cases I know well, the time and effort spent on refocusing from poor work to good work reflect many years of operations where work standards were lax. Today, companies find themselves in highly competitive situations and must refocus the energy of the organization on new highs of quality.

When you look closely at cases, the emphasis of many quality management efforts is on cheerleading and persuasion, which aim to change the culture from a parochial view of work to an effectiveness ethic. If you adopt the EP process of productivity management, the recommended action steps will cause a natural focus on customer needs and high-quality work, without massive special efforts or additional staff specialists.

The recommended EP process starts with efforts to create an effectiveness ethic and a productivity culture. Productivity management is assigned to all managers who must respond to the needs of their customers, inside or outside the company. And with this method, how well these things are done is measured. It is the measures that address the issue of focus. Productivity measures should reflect high quality and satisfaction of customer requirements.

A Mixed Workforce

Another facet of restructuring involves the more effective use of a mixed workforce. In a mixed workforce, some of the work is done by people who are not full-time employees. This is a version of outsourcing and has grown a lot in the past decade, mostly as a result of striving for higher productivity.

Those in a mixed workforce can be contract workers, part-time workers, temporary employees, or leased workers. In some cases, the proper use of such workers can contribute substantially to greater productivity.

In fact, all companies have a mixed workforce to some extent. Public accountants and outside lawyers are contract workers. As a consultant, I earned my living as a contract worker. Security guards, catered restaurant operations, and part-time employee organizations are big businesses. Almost one in ten people at work today is in the mixed workforce.

Essentially, outsourcing makes it possible to get the best people for a job at a favorable cost, and you only use them when you need them. Such conditions often contribute to more effective work. Many of these people could not be used economically on a full-time basis and would not accept such a job anyway. But the smallest company can hire the best contract worker on an as-needed basis. Some of those contract workers are very expensive. But the work they do is worth a lot. Sometimes you have to use their services, for example, when you need an actuary. However, you don't have to put them on the payroll, and if they become too costly, you can simplify or eliminate the programs that require their work.

In some ways, workers who are not full-time are the most cost-effective, regardless of price, because you only use them when you need them. There is never a question of finding work for them to do; you just don't use them.

Another reason for hiring contract labor has to do with the difficulties and cost of having employees on the payroll. That, too, is a productivity-related reason for contract workers.

Companies outsource work because the pay rates are lower in the contracting firm, or the work is done more effectively. In either case, outsourcing results in improved productivity.

Using people from a mixed workforce involves make-or-buy decisions. More and more man-hours of work are purchased because that is the cost-effective thing to do. All of this is restructuring by manpower management. The company is choosing not only the best workers for a job but also the best type of worker.

Always remember that whatever category they're in, all workers affect productivity and cost just like your regular full-time employees. All employees, whether on the company payroll or from a mixed workforce, impact productivity and customer satisfaction.

Manpower Management and Rightsizing

For too many years, the management of manpower has been long periods of gradual increases and periodic purges and drastic reductions. The growth is gradual, and each added job seems to be a good idea that doesn't cost very much. Generally over time, the result is organizational fat, which must be eliminated.

Increases in staff happened a case at a time and over a period of time. Logically then, downsizing should best be handled a case at a time and over a period of time. It doesn't happen like that, however, because downsizing is driven by needs to reduce cost in one accounting period, and downsizing needs, therefore, tend to be immediate needs.

Organizational fatness occurred because work was added, then jobs had to be created, and staff was added to do the work. Then it would be reasonable to accomplish downsizing by eliminating unneeded work and, in time, eliminating jobs and the workers who did those jobs.

Downsizing has of late been a media story and a very important business story. This is legitimate, although the reasons for it have not been reported well. Only a portion of downsizing has occurred from getting rid of unneeded jobs or excessive manpower. Downsizing has mostly happened because of organizational streamlining, eliminating unproductive practices, and substituting computer and computer-related machines for human physical and mental effort. These actions have been productivity improvement efforts. They have been effective in increasing productivity, and the visible result was downsizing.

Productivity means more work with fewer people. Productivity improvement will mean layoffs. Productivity improvement will mean that the national product will grow faster than employment increases.

Excessive manpower is always a productivity issue. Upsizing followed by downsizing should be avoided. Instead, institute manpower management practices that result in rightsizing. Many have wrestled with the problems of manpower management and rightsizing. Monumental studies have been made over the years. There have been many failures, but there have also been successes. Based on the successes, I recommend the following to clients regarding an ongoing manpower management effort.

+ The key to successful manpower management is *information*. In this computer age, a great deal of information is available to indicate correct compliment levels in every section of an organization and under every condition. Such information should be available to those who make manpower decisions.
+ One important piece of information is productivity measures. If productivity is increasing at a good rate, manpower is a secondary consideration and rarely an issue. If productivity trends are disappointing, look closely to see if there is a manpower problem. If productivity is flat or declining, there is a problem, and it's likely that at least part of the problem is excessive manpower.
+ Manning tables and complement ratios of all types are very helpful. Make sure that this data is based in part on best past experience, not just numbers on paper.
+ Every staff and support activity should be subjected to some type of activity value analysis at least once every five years. Don't be ruthless, but be from Missouri, and make staff and support people prove that what they do is necessary.

12

Performance Management

Performance management is productivity action step 11. Remember that performance, productivity, and operating results are quite different. However, performance is clearly a major part of productivity, and productivity is a major determinant of operating results.

Performance must always be a consideration in productivity work because of the clear relationship between the effectiveness of the work of each individual and the output per man-hour of a group. That's why I recommend performance management as a specific productivity action step.

Performance management involves the effective management of people. There are special practices essential to managing people, and these are matching, appraisal, and training. Performance management is also dealing with specific workers and specific incidents day by day. High performance depends upon a form of operational leadership excellence.

Managing

To a large extent, it seems clear that it is the managers of people who largely determine the performance of those workers. This seems obvious, and yet it is so important to productivity management that it is worth saying. Based on this assumption, the way to get higher performance and ultimately higher productivity and better business results is by having more effective managers.

More effective managing has always been an important part of my productivity improvement work. To do this, I have spent a lot of my time and the time of my associates learning as much as possible about managing. I had an advantage because I managed three businesses in my career. Furthermore, I worked deeply enough with hundreds of companies in consulting to learn something about how the managers of these companies performed.

My conclusion from all of this learning is that there are no real experts on managing, partly because there are so many ways to manage effectively. The practice of managing people must be personalized—to the manager and to those managed.

Many of the people represented as experts in managing are really experts in personnel management, as I am. But personnel management is about personnel techniques and practices and only indirectly relates to managing people. Personnel management and the management of personnel are not the same thing.

Many techniques have been developed to help a person become a better manager of people. These techniques are often clever, like the managerial grid, or they are psychologically based, so they seem to have academic endorsement. These techniques of managing may be helpful as tools to promote the better management of people, but they are always costly and have sometimes been harmful.

Various practices have been designed to reflect the one best way of doing some task of managing people, and these methods have been thought to be helpful in improving performance. Management by objectives, for example, emphasizes setting specific goals and measuring success against them. Such practices may be helpful to some managers under some conditions, but they represent just one from among many effective ways of managing.

All these techniques and practices may help to improve managing. They may also keep some from managing better, or force everyone toward managing at a level of mediocrity. Whatever the values and issues relating to the techniques and practices, they aren't managing. They are only attempts to assist, improve, control, or dictate the practices of managing.

There may be no one way to manage well, but here are some suggestions:

- Pay a lot of attention to the selection of people for first-time management assignments. At this point you are looking for the types of attributes that seem to predict success in managing.
- Consider whether the person likes to do managing work and why.
- After the first management assignment, select people for subsequent promotions to higher level management jobs at least in part by how well they have managed people in the past.
- Work to establish effective networks for managers, particularly with other managers of people.
- Measure the managers' performance by the performance of the workers they manage. Make sure they know this, and make sure their pay is dependent in part upon how well their subordinates perform.
- Provide direct, usable, accessible support when it is needed and asked for.

Aside from these commonsense guidelines, performance management should focus on four areas:

- Matching
- Appraisal of performance
- Jobs training
- Close attention to the superstars and effective reactions to the problem employees

Matching

Matching involves assigning people to jobs. Today, matching also often means restructuring jobs or changing organizations to utilize the talent of the people available to do the work—matching jobs to people.

Employees are not interchangeable parts. So what people can do and how those talents are deployed to get needed work done are important to the effectiveness of work.

Matching is a continuous job. The nature of the work or

schedules may change, and new assignments must be made. There are absences or there are work problems, and this changes the work to be done and work assignments. An employee might have a special problem and need a different assignment. Someone might get sick at work or have to leave, and that means rematching. All such considerations require matching decisions.

If you have never managed an operation, you may not appreciate the extent of assignments and reassignments. There are dozens, hundreds, or thousands of instances every year per employee in a work group. A small work group of ten employees could easily mean a thousand matching decisions yearly.

Matching greatly affects productivity. Assigning the best available person to each job makes an obvious difference in work effectiveness. Handling each of these matching instances even somewhat better can improve productivity measurably.

It isn't just a matter of assigning a person who can do a job and not assigning a person who can't do the job. Matching means assigning all workers in the group to get the maximum effectiveness, having the best deployment of talent. People's reasonable interests as well as their qualifications must be considered. Job assignments can't be a cold mechanical process. People's reasonable preferences are part of effective matching, because we do best what we like to do.

Effective matching often requires job redesign, which involves restructuring jobs. One major reason for job restructuring is to better utilize the talent of the people who are available. Effective matching might also involve changing an employee so his or her talent is in line with the work requirements. "Changing" an employee might mean training, transfer, or providing new tools or accessories. Matching may require broadening the know-how and skills of the people in a work group to provide needed flexibility for effective matching.

Matching is an art and a skill. It is a skill in managing. You must know the work to be done, and you must know the capabilities of the people who are available to do the work. Then you must work hard at matching.

There are no set principles or guidelines that can be learned and then used to improve matching. Each decision must be made by the person who manages the operation. Furthermore, most matching decisions must be made immediately, without benefit of deep thinking, evaluation, and careful reflection.

Matching is an operating manager's job. Even the most talented corporate staff cannot do this work well, as General Foods found out. For a number of years, General Foods had a "job enrichment" department in the corporate personnel organization. Job enrichment was largely a matter of matching. General Foods assigned this work to very high level human resources people and committed significant resources to the project. After about five years, however, the effort was discontinued. It was a good attempt by talented people to get better matching throughout the company, but was an impossible task for the corporate staff because they didn't know the work well enough to add anything of value to the matching processes that were occurring hundreds of times every hour in the operations.

Performance Appraisal

If you are to manage performance, it is essential to know how good a person's performance is and to understand how his or her performance might be better. It is in this sense that performance appraisal is an integral part of performance management and, therefore, productivity management.

It's as simple as this: If you don't know what each person's performance level is, you can't really manage performance. That means you must rate each employee's performance in some way. It's also true that in order to take intelligent actions to improve performance, it is necessary to evaluate current performance enough to understand how it can be improved, if at all. This means that there must be some form of evaluative performance appraisal to determine how to improve performance.

To get performance ratings and to evaluate performance to determine appropriate action steps to improve it require some form of appraisal. Performance appraisal is a vital management practice because it gets ratings and involves evaluating action steps to improve performance.

Some colleagues whom I respect highly say that performance appraisal does not work. What they mean is that the performance appraisal system in their company doesn't work. In fact, performance appraisal programs in many companies don't work well. They often fail because they are too complex and don't support sound performance ratings and the evaluation of performance to determine action steps to improve individual employee efforts.

I recommend with confidence the following guidelines for an effective performance appraisal program that will support productivity management:

1. Current performance on the job must be rated in a numeric rating on a maximum of five gradients. No explanation or analysis is required. The rating conclusion is fed into corporate headquarters as part of the human resources information system.

2. There must be evaluative appraisal of each person to determine how his or her performance could be improved. From this evaluation, specific actions are determined to improve performance. These should be done for every case that is relevant, but it is not required for every person. You should expect one or a maximum of two planned action steps for at least two-thirds of all employees, and you should expect that at least one-third of them will be successful. That level of performance improvement represents a substantial improvement in productivity.

3. The performance appraisal system should do nothing but rate performance and require evaluative appraisal to determine action steps to improve effectiveness. That doesn't mean nothing else should be done, just that nothing else should be done as part of this performance appraisal process.

4. Never *require* feedback of the results of this appraisal process unless an employee specifically asks for it. Of course, a manager should let every employee know how well he or she is doing, but that should be done incident by incident all the time and not in a once-a-year, formal system.

5. Don't require that anything other than a numeric conclusion about performance level be sent to a headquarters office or to any personnel department.

6. Don't use a form or ask a lot of performance-related questions.
7. Whenever performance ratings remain below a satisfactory level or decline, have human resources people make a thorough investigation and determine the cause.

These guidelines describe a system of performance appraisal that is *guaranteed* to contribute to high levels of performance. This system is much less costly than most of those used in business, gets higher levels of support from operating managers, is accepted by employees, and is excellent in compliance cases. Most of all, it contributes substantially to higher productivity.

Training

Training on the job is an integral part of performance management and may contribute significantly to greater productivity. Any type of training or training-related activity that improves work effectiveness contributes to greater productivity and better job performance.

Some people think that training is so important that it should be a separate, stand-alone action step in productivity management. The advantage of having training as part of performance management is to keep the work focused on improving performance on the job now.

Jobs Training

There are many different types of training activities. In productivity management the issue is jobs training, and more specifically, only what training is needed to improve performance. Training-related activities such as development and additional education have great values for a business and the workforce, but they are mostly activities to prepare employees for future assignments. Behavior modification training may also have some use, but not in performance management work. I have often challenged the providers of behavioral development activities to prove that their programs improve performance, but they have never been able to show me any correlation between behavior modification and work excellence.

There are performance improvement training sessions. Many are fancy and entertaining, but they all tend to be a single technique or practice of work that everyone is supposed to learn. They may have some value, but I think jobs training must be highly customized to each person's needs.

Every person is different with respect to talent and ability. Increasingly in a work environment of rapid change and higher technology, what each person knows and what he or she needs to learn can vary a great deal. Furthermore, in more and more workplaces, the need for individual job training can be different today than it was even a short time ago, and tomorrow's needs are largely unpredictable.

These conditions increasingly describe the jobs training needs in business. Government and business must gear their actions accordingly. For most companies, this means a heavy emphasis on operational training.

Operational Training

In the workplace, operational training goes on all the time. A person doesn't know how to do something and is shown. A person does an assignment and then is shown how to do that work better the next time. A worker does some assignment differently and it works better or it work less well. Every incident can be a learning experience, not only for one person but for others in the work group. It is the hundreds or thousands of variations of experiences that in combination make up operational training.

Clearly, the operating managers must do a lot of the operational training, or see to it that work needs are identified and met by special training. This work obviously places a very heavy responsibility on all operating managers. They often cannot do the operating training job well and need instruction and guidance. But who is qualified to train the trainers?

In my productivity management work, I focused heavily on trying to develop operations training, to do things that would make it just somewhat better. What worked best was to select managers who did operations training well and employees who wanted to do better. For many years I looked for someone who was truly expert in operations training, but I have never found that person. It seems to me that there is a great need to have access to experts in operations training.

Keep telling managers to do operations training well. Urge them in every way to train better and better. Make sure they have every possible available resource. I never found anything else I could recommend that would enrich or improve operational training.

Programmed Training

There are times when some training needs can be met most effectively by a training session. For example, sometimes a number of people have the same need for training to enhance effectiveness of their work. In such situations, some type of programmatic training may be the right thing to do.

Some urge the use of productivity training sessions. These would be formal sessions that teach workers how to be more effective or that teach methods to become more productive. You have to judge each course on its own merits.

Productivity sessions can be useful in communicating the need for greater productivity. Sessions conducted by a motivational speaker might contribute to more of an effectiveness ethic. Learning about productivity actions steps or techniques that have been used might also be useful.

There are also sessions that promise to make people more productive. Organizational development made that promise for years. Now TQM sessions are said to result in greater effectiveness of work. You might consider such sessions, though my observed experiences suggest that they don't work.

Some productivity improvement systems rely heavily on behavior modification training to change people's attitudes toward work and to create some type of a productivity culture. Some have been very fancy and have had enthusiastic sponsors. Developing a productivity culture is one of the required action steps in the EP process. But I have never seen this brought about by a training system, and I have seen many attempts to do so.

As much as anything, I have always urged companies to recognize that it is operational training that mostly brings about improved employee performance. Therefore, that should be emphasis. If some program seems to have potential usefulness as a supplement to operations training, use it. But never place the focus of training on programmatic training.

Distinguished Employees and Problem Employees

The performance of every worker is important to the level of productivity and operating results. But the performance of the most outstanding workers justifies particular focus, and the performance of problem employees takes disproportionate amounts of time. The superstars and the problem employees are particular issues of performance management.

Distinguished employees are those who are always in the highest performance category. They are the best in their class or group.

Distinguished performers directly contribute to high productivity through their own effectiveness. In addition, the tone and standards they set indirectly affect the productivity of others. These employees are the pacesetters. They show what can be done. They develop better ways and resolve difficult issues. Distinguished employees account for a very large portion of innovation, progress, problem solving, and new ideas in any organization. The rule of thumb I use is that the top 10 percent performers are responsible for 90 percent of the operational improvement.

Effective performance management requires careful attention to distinguished employees. A quit by one of these distinguished employees is a serious business loss. They are invaluable assets that are difficult to replace.

Make sure you understand the goals and the gripes of these employees. Keep them challenged, provide proper recognition, and be very sure that their compensation progress reflects the high levels of their performance.

Problem employees detract from effectiveness. One goal in working with problem employees is to improve their performance and to end detractions from productivity. The problem employee detracts mostly by poor performance, by causing trouble, and by involving a high cost.

There are three general types of problem employees, and they involve very different situations. These are:

- Those who are problems because of work-related issues.
- Those who are problems because of conditions or circumstances.
- Those who are problems because of their behavior or social preferences.

The work-related problem employees are the traditional problem employees, and organizations should be pretty good at dealing with them. Essentially, dealing with work-related problems is the job of the manager.

Conditions-related problem workers are those whose performance is low or costs are high because of their special circumstances. They aren't bad people or even poor workers; they just have conditions that detract from their performance or add to their cost, or both. This includes functionally illiterate workers, some disabled workers, and some women with young children. Clearly, handling these problems is not only difficult but involves sensitive matters and compliance issues.

The third and newest type of major performance problem employees are those related to behavior. These include such areas as engaging in sexual harassment, using drugs, and being a radical member of a special interest group. These people cause disruptions and problems in the workplace even when their performance is good.

How these problem employees are handled is clearly a determinant of effectiveness. If these employees are handled poorly or if their problems are unresolved, performance will be lower. Better management of problem employees (which means they are less of a problem) contributes to better performance and higher productivity.

One-Day-at-a-Time Management

Day-to-day operating management greatly affects performance results. Each work incident has a potential impact on performance. If you have never managed a group of people, you really can't appreciate how much the performance of workers is determined by events and incidents that happen daily. Unfortunately, many staff persons who work on matters of effective productivity and some experts who are widely followed have never managed people or have done so in a very limited manner or in a sterile environment.

The absences, antagonisms, equipment breakdowns, shortages, personnel problems, questions, complaints, and all the other things that happen on a continuous basis represent an avalanche of incidents, each of which may affect the performance of one person, a number of people, or a whole group. The manager faces a continuing list of issues, questions, and problems. They are often unique and sometimes difficult. It is easy to make a mistake, partly because things usually have to be done right away without benefit of all the facts and without time for careful analysis.

I once heard an industrial engineer estimate that each incident involving work affected the overall productivity of a work group an average of .001 percent. No one asked how he got that number because it seemed so small, but his point was that individual cases didn't really make much of a difference in the productivity of an organization (and, of course, industrial engineering made a big difference). But by the same analytic method used to come up with that .001 percent, I determined that there is an average of two such incidents per employee per workday; about 3,500 incidents per employee per year. If the company in this case had 10,000 employees, there would be 35 million day-to-day work incidents affecting productivity each year. This could mean that one-day-at-a-time management could affect performance up to 35 percent per year.

In fact, some decisions regarding day-to-day matters affect performance positively and others affect performance negatively. But if you could increase your positive decisions affecting performance from 50 to 55 percent, then performance and, theoretically, productivity would improve.

Each incident has the potential to affect performance. Each incident sets a precedent that affects future incidents. All of these represent an important part of performance management. How these day-to-day incidents are handled has a great effect on people's performance and on the productivity of the operation. One-day-at-a-time management is critical to high performance and increasing productivity.

Operating Leadership

In performance management, the leadership needed is among the operating managers. Executive leadership impacts business results and productivity, but executives have mostly a policy impact on performance. If it is correct that leadership by operating managers impacts performance, then improved leadership will improve performance. Here are thoughts and suggestions about how to improve operating leadership.

From my studies and experiences, I conclude that *operating* leadership is generally quite good whenever operating management has been judged to be competent. That suggests that successful managers have natural leadership qualities or acquire leadership qualities on their own.

Don't think that you can create leadership when it doesn't exist. However, in many cases, actions can be taken to improve operating leadership. But the improvement will not be certain and will rarely be dramatic.

Leadership improvement is very cost-ineffective work. You should not consider work to improve operating leadership unless the leadership is poor and you can be reasonably sure that improved leadership will result in a distinct improvement in performance.

The simplest and surest way to improve operating leadership is to start now to select people for manager positions who have demonstrated leadership qualities. Create conditions that facilitate more exercise of leadership, such as more delegative management. And let the operating managers know that it is part of their job to exercise leadership.

Leadership, like intelligence, is mostly an innate quality. You can get people to exploit the abilities they have, but you can't change genes and create new abilities.

There are those who claim to be able to develop leadership

qualities through training programs. I have never seen that happen, but we should always keep an open mind.

Good leadership of leaders makes them better leaders. An operating manager learns about leadership when managed by a good leader and is often inspired to do more leading among his or her subordinates. Make sure that there is understanding about what operating leadership qualities are, and then focus your attention on these attributes, to the extent you can.

There is some disagreement about leadership attributes among operating managers. I recommend four threshold attributes of operating management leadership:

- Manager must have high levels of credibility among those who work for them.
- Managers must be reasonably good at their own work, aside from managing.
- Managers must have a positive, can-do attitude.
- Managers must be personally acceptable by their subordinates, not necessarily liked but respected and not thought to be obnoxious.

An operating manager must have all of these attributes if he or she is to have leadership talent. In addition, an operating manager-leader will have some attributes that are highly unique and personal. The additional attribute may be as diverse as charisma or a reputation for personal excellence. The additional attribute may or may not be directly work related (such as the manager might have been a war hero).

When you consider these matters, you may conclude that the four required attributes are qualities that you should insist on having in every supervisor. Then focus on selecting or highlighting the additional personal attribute, and the individual does things to take advantage of that attribute.

Performance management requires attention to all of the elements identified in this chapter: day-to-day management, matching, appraisal, training, handling the superstars and the problem employees, and leadership. Performance alone does not determine productivity levels, but it is important enough to make performance management a separate action step in the EP method.

13

Pay for Performance

This is the twelfth and last step in the EP process of productivity management. Where there is an opportunity to perform better, there should be pay for performance. Pay for performance can be a powerful force in achieving high levels of work effectiveness.

Only pay for performance that relates to productivity is covered in this chapter. For more about compensation, I recommend that you read *Compensation*.*

A Brief on Pay and Productivity

With rare exceptions, it is not possible to link pay directly with productivity. Therefore, productivity pay plans are impractical. They are not practical usually because productivity data lack the precision required to link pay and productivity. Furthermore, premium pay is a reward for personal accomplishment. Yet a great deal of productivity improvement comes from capital substitution, and workers do not contribute to most of the productivity resulting from that.

I have often been asked to develop productivity pay systems. Such efforts were never successful, and I have yet to see a successful productivity pay plan in my thirty-three years of consulting.

Because productivity pay plans are not practical, we link pay

*Robert E. Sibson, *Compensation*, 5th ed., AMACOM, New York, 1990.

to performance. Performance can be measured for a person or a group. Furthermore, people have at least some control of their own performance. Because performance and productivity are linked, performance pay rewards employees for their contribution to greater productivity when there is pay for performance.

To be successful, certain requirements for performance pay are suggested by experience. Seven broad guidelines for effective pay for performance are listed below.

1. There must be an intelligent and clear definition of performance.
2. Pay for performance clearly motivates people, so recognize that it is not only fair to pay more to those who produce more but that such a system will get people to be more productive.
3. Employees overwhelmingly think that pay for performance is fair.
4. Higher than competitive pay based on better performance is, or should be, a zero cost to the employer.
5. The pay premium for better-than-average performance must be linked to the amount of greater output.
6. There are proven and practical plans to implement a pay for performance policy.
7. You can expect some objections and many questions about pay for performance.

Each of these seven pay for performance guidelines are covered in more detail in the following sections. Except for specific plan information, these data should be sufficient for designing your own pay for performance system and for implementing this productivity action step.

Definition

One of the biggest single problems with performance pay and performance management is reaching a broad agreement about what is meant by the word "performance." It should mean how well a person does his or her assigned job, and nothing else.

Pay for performance means more pay for better performance on an assigned job. Everyone should be expected to perform to standard and acceptable levels of work after they have training and the required experience. That level of performance gets market pay. Performance above standard gets higher pay.

After there is a common understanding of what performance means, there are two performance pay issues. First, there is the question of whether performance levels can be determined. Second, there must be an acceptance of the fact that there will not be extra pay for anything other than performance.

Obviously, the ability to determine performance levels is essential in pay for performance. If you can't distinguish between levels of performance, you cannot gear pay to performance. That gets to the question of whether managers can judge differences in performance levels and whether they will do that correctly and with integrity in such a system.

Of course, managers know performance levels and performance differences. I have always been amazed when this issue was raised. If a manager does not know the differences in the performance of subordinates, you could argue that that manager does not manage.

Managers have the ability to determine performance levels and, in fact, they do it without urging all the time. They use this knowledge regularly in directing work in the organizational unit. What often happens is that many managers are reluctant to supply performance information to unknown persons elsewhere in the company for unknown purposes. Many managers also wonder why anyone at corporate headquarters would want the information requested in performance appraisal programs, and they worry about how it might be used. Under these circumstances, there is a natural disinclination to supply performance information, whether it is favorable or unfavorable.

There have been cases where the information requested in performance appraisal forms *has* been used improperly, or in a manner that reasonable managers would think was not helpful. It is the details of the information requested that has caused mangers to be reluctant about sending this information to headquarters, not these managers' lack of knowledge about the performance levels of those who work in their organization.

Pay for performance may not be for any of the following reasons:

- Length of service or seniority
- Attendance or punctuality
- Personal views or opinions about anything
- Appearance
- Greater skills
- More knowledge
- Race, sex, or age
- Cooperativeness, friendliness, likability, or any other personal trait
- Good interpersonal relationships or being a good member of some team

You could make a very long list of attributes that should not be rewarded by pay increases under a pay for performance system of compensation. Pay each job competitively, and then pay more to those who perform above average or expected, based solely on performance.

There will always be pressure to grant salary increases for reasons such as those listed above. These reasons will often seem fair and perhaps even compelling to some people. There are those who think it is fair and just to pay people for long service. They will tell you that higher pay is a proper reward for long service and that such a practice encourages people to stay with the company. You could debate these arguments, but recognize that there is merit in such thinking. The real argument relating to length of service increases is that such extra payments may make it less possible or impossible to pay more money for better performance.

In this technological world, some people argue for skills pay. They think that if people have more skills, the employer is better off. Of course, if they are correct, these greater skills will show up in better performance. But aside from the merits and problems of the pay for skills view, if such payments result in inadequate funds for reward of performance, this thinking cannot be tolerated.

There is some merit in each basis of payment listed, but they are not reflected in performance or in the ability of the company to attract and retain the talent needed to run the operations. Only competitiveness and performance should determine pay.

Motivation

As long as I have been in personnel work, various authorities have claimed that pay does not motivate. Many psychologists and some well-known people in the personnel field maintain in some way to differing degrees that pay does not motivate or at least not motivate very much.

The first time I heard this argument was in 1953, when Professor Herzberg, a leading motivational expert, gave a speech to the New York Personnel Management Association. His view, based on some research at a few companies, was that unfair pay can demotivate but that pay linked to performance was not a motivator. However, all twelve people at my table agreed that pay motivated us a lot. One of them was on the speaker's committee and said that the association had to raise the standard speaker's fee to get Professor Herzberg to talk to the group, so pay motivated him, too.

Later, when working on organizational problems for General Mills, I learned that their chief operating officer was a big Herzberg fan. Because of this, I had to do some research on Herzberg's work to determine what led him to his widely publicized conclusions. It turned out that Herzberg had looked at the experiences of only seven companies. Each either had no pay for performance program or the pay plans they did have were poor by any professional standard of compensation.

There are plenty of companies without pay for performance plans and many others with poor plans. Make your own studies. Ask people you know if pay motivates them, or if pay really linked to performance would make a difference in what they did. What you will find is that almost everyone will work at least somewhat differently if they are paid on the basis of what they do. If they are paid for performance, they will perform somewhat better to get more pay, if that is possible.

If you need more evidence about the effect of pay on performance, look at the commission pay plans for salespeople and piecework pay plans for factory workers. Data always show that people produce more when their pay is linked to their output. There won't always be dramatic changes or extreme responses to performance pay. That sometimes happens, but the changes often occur gradually over time. The changes are sometimes subtle. People just reorder their priorities or focus somewhat more on the needs of the business.

My view of pay and motivation is this: For most people, during most of their working lives, pay may not be the only thing, but it is way ahead of whatever it is that is in second place.

Fairness

Working people overwhelmingly think that pay for performance is fair. Even less effective workers who would be disadvantaged by a pay for performance system think that pay for performance is the right thing to do.

Of course, working people at every level want *more*. They will support every type of raise for any reason as long as the employer does not run out of money. But if the funds are limited and if the employer is to give a pay increase on the basis of performance or something else, employees will overwhelmingly think it's right to do it on the basis of performance.

The results of our mainstream survey of employee attitudes,* conducted in 1992, showed that four of five employees clearly favor pay for performance. Two-thirds of these workers also said that management did not pay for performance nearly as much as it should.

Many cases have been reported where employees were said to be opposed to performance pay. In every instance I have seen, the organization *said* that pay increases were for performance or merit, but, in fact, they were for something else. These were often discretionary pay plans, where the managers alone decided what the increase was for each person. The increases were actually for many things, but they were all called merit increases.

*See Appendix B.

However, the merit could be related to loyalty to that manager or to a certain type of behavior that the manager favored. Many of the so-called merit increase plans of the past were partially discretionary. All stated that the pay increases were for merit, but that meant they were *merited*. Very often they were merited because of highly discretionary reasons.

Don't think that all performance pay plans have failed. There have been many success cases, but they have mostly been in small or moderate-size companies. In these success cases, the salary increases were only for inflation or performance.

Employees support pay for performance partly because it reflects equal pay for equal work. If two people do the same job equally well, they should be paid the same. If one of these people produces more work, then equal pay means that person must be paid more.

Pay for performance must be applied consistently and under all circumstances. If one person is rewarded for performance, then everyone should be rewarded, and to an equivalent degree. There can be no exceptions in applying pay for performance. There must be pay for performance in good times and in bad times.

Pay for performance increases cannot be limited by salary increase budgets, which limit the amount of performance improvement desired or permitted. Companies can use all the improved performance they can get, and they must reward performance improvement by performance salary increases.

Zero Cost

Pay for performance is fair for the employer not only because it motivates people to perform better, satisfies the better performers, and is regarded by most employees as being fair, but also because performance pay increases cost nothing. Pay for performance is free.

As an employee's performance improves, the output of that employee increases. As output increases, revenues are greater or costs are lower. The same number of employees produce more, or the same work is produced by fewer employees. In either case, or by any combination of output and cost, genuine improvement in performance costs nothing as long as the revenues increase or the cost savings are at least as great as the pay increase.

Actually, if pay increases are equal to performance improvement, the company makes money, partially because of reduced overhead. Thus pay increases that equal performance increases are not only free, but there is a return on the expenditure. This makes pay increases based on performance an investment, and the return on the investment is received by the employer before the investment (the pay increase) is made to the employee. That is a truly unique investment for any employer.

Pay for performance can be in the form of a salary reward for performance plan, a bonus plan, or a success-sharing plan. In each of these plans, true pay for performance costs nothing. (Individual plans are discussed later under Effective Pay for Performance Plans.)

Pay motivates and contributes to greater performance and ultimately greater productivity. Pay for performance is fair to everyone involved, the company, the employees, and the owners. And pay for performance doesn't cost anything.

Performance Spread and Pay Spread

Premium pay for better than standard or expected performance should equate to the amount of the premium performance. The differences in pay above competitive market levels should reflect the differences in performance above standard or expected levels of performance typical in labor markets. If the employee's performance is 10 percent above standard, then his or her pay should be 10 percent above market average. It is often prudent to have a pay differential that is only a part of the performance spread, however. For example, if the performance spread is 20 percent, the pay spread might be only 10 percent. The reason is because the pay premium is definite, whereas the performance spread is often judgmental.

Recognize that in some jobs there is no difference in performance. The performance spread is zero, and everyone is expected to perform about the same. Airline pilots is an example.

In jobs where differences in output are due primarily to

physical attributes and effort, the spread between acceptable and optimum performance is rarely more than 30 percent. In many knowledge jobs, the difference in performance among professionals, even at the same level of professional work, can be more than 100 percent.

Very often there are considerable difficulties in setting the performance spread with precision. The commonsense answer is to make sure that each case of better performance can actually be described as better and then require a significantly greater performance spread than pay spread.

Don't be overly concerned about details or being perfect. Concentrate on rewarding performance with more pay. Make sure that this principle is followed and that employees believe that pay is for competitive market reasons or for performance.

Effective Pay for Performance Plans

Many plans are available to employers for implementing pay for performance. Not having an effective pay for performance plan should never be due to an absence of a workable plan or unsolved technical issues. Those without pay for performance have chosen some other view, or they have not had the will to implement pay for performance.

A number of plans have been used successfully by many companies for many years. They can include a salary reward, a bonus plan, or a success-sharing plan.

With respect to salary reward for performance, the critical plan provision is that somehow the plan must clearly identify the pay increase that is made for improved performance. That means a separate pay increase for performance or that an identifiable portion of some increase is specifically earmarked for performance.

Salary increases labeled as performance pay increases must clearly be for improved performance and *only* for improved performance. Employees must believe that such increases are plainly for that and nothing else.

For a performance pay increase program to be effective, it must work. That means the pay system must not only reward better performance but also contribute to greater performance in some significant manner. The plan must be simple for this to happen. The plan must be understandable to the employees. The plan must plainly reward for better performance.

To achieve these objectives, there must be a minimum pay increase amount that roughly equates to the minimum amount of the performance improvement that is observable and explainable. Experience suggests that this is at least 7 percent, and perhaps as much as 12 percent. If this is correct, any amount much less than 7 percent is not for performance improvement, no matter what is said.

I emphasize that performance pay cannot be contingent upon any factor other than performance. It cannot be dependent on any salary increase budget or on the economic circumstances of the times. Employees must be certain that if their performance improves significantly, they will receive a performance salary increase. This means that companies will pay performance salary increases in good times and in bad times. They will pay performance salary increases in areas of the business that are losing money as well as in those that are doing well. *Any* artificial limit or restriction on performance salary increases will mean that it is not a performance salary pay plan.

The mechanisms of salary administration are less important than these basic principles and requirements. In fact, a number of salary systems work well. The one characteristic common to all of the good performance pay systems is that there is a salary increase when performance increases in amounts that can be described and proven.

Many different types of bonus plans have also been used effectively in many companies to reward group performance. The key to such plans is the excellence of the performance goals.

These goals should always be specific and numeric. For example, the performance standards for paying a bonus might be linked to approved budgets.

All bonus plans must be paid on top of the proper salary, which is competitive salary plus salary reward for performance. Any bonus plan will be less effective than it should be or even ineffective unless it is based on this principle. Group bonus plans should be geared to group goals. The best practice is to pay bonus amounts only for exceeding standard or budgeted goals. This important principle means that bonus payments represent extra pay for extra achievements by the group.

Bonus amounts earned by achieving or exceeding performance standards must be paid. Company financial results cannot be the basis for withholding bonus amounts earned.

A success-sharing plan is pay for the achievements of the organization overall. As long as the basis for success sharing is somehow limited to long-term improvement in operations, these payments may also be said to cost the employer nothing.

Designing performance pay plans is not always easy, and an organization may have to seek help. But there are many sound plans to consider. Performance pay is a powerful productivity management action step. In fact, for the company that wants a simplified productivity improvement system, I would recommend the adoption of the first four essentials of productivity management and the implementation of a pay for performance system. This would set the essentials for improving productivity and would be an incentive for managers and workers throughout the organization to do it.

Objections

Why doesn't every company have a pay for performance plan? Too often the answer is that the plans are flawed or an employer has pay increases for some other factor beside performance, leaving insufficient money to pay for performance.

14

Doing Productivity Management Work

If you conclude that there should be an organized effort in your organization to increase productivity by the EP method outlined in the previous chapters, the next step is to determine how to proceed. Each organization has its own culture and its own way of doing things. However, there are sound guidelines in productivity management work that are worth considering.

First, determine clearly and factually the need to do productivity improvement work. Get detailed data about the potential gain from productivity and the cost of doing the work. Be specific about what will be accomplished and why that is important to the organization.

Then determine the method of productivity management. Of course, I recommend that you adopt some variation of the EP approach. If you do, there will be identifiable phases of work and action steps to be determined. Other problems and issues must be considered, too. None is more important than evolving a continuing productivity improvement effort in your organization.

The important thing is to get started. This is simple if you use the EP process; simplicity is one of the many advantages of this approach.

EP—A Step at a Time

If you decide to apply the EP process of productivity management, the only *required* work involves the first four basic steps described in Chapters 2 through 5. You *must* get executive commitment, develop a productivity culture, assign the productivity management job to operating managers, and establish productivity measures.

These basic actions take a moderate amount of time and involve a modest cost, but they are all natural management actions. There are no special or unusual practices. There are no new concepts to learn and no different practices to master. You don't have to attend training sessions to understand these methods. In the four basic steps of the EP process that *must* be applied, you just use natural management methods. Most specifically, the application of these four steps is not personnel work or total quality management work. It is nothing more or less than managing.

It is a great advantage for every company to be able to take on the productivity management job in manageable steps. The first four required action steps are a very manageable job in most organizations. Generally, a moderate-size organization with 500 to 2,500 employees in a number of locations could apply these first four steps in as little as six months. Any size firm, no matter how large, could apply these first four steps in one year.

There is no need to hire extra people or to have specialists do these basic four steps in the EP process. No one needs a consultant to help implement the steps. Implement these four action steps *first*. Don't try to take all twelve steps at the same time. Only after the basic action steps have been accomplished should you consider the other steps. I list eight additional action steps beyond the basic four in this book. Although these are the most widely applied, other steps might be useful in individual circumstances. Implement *some* of these steps after the basic steps. Choose those that have the greatest impact on productivity in your organization. Also pick the action steps that are the most likely to be successful.

It is at this point that you are customizing the EP process to your own company. Pick the action steps that will work the best for you. Pick one or more, whatever makes sense and whatever you think your organization can handle.

I have found that it's much better to do a few productivity action steps at a time and to do them well. Don't yield to the temptation to pick many steps and proceed on a grand scale. There is no advantage in doing this, and the more you take on, the greater the chance of difficulties and even failure.

As you work on whatever steps you choose, there will be a time when each has run its course, or the improvement in productivity due to these action steps is slowing down. When this happens, do two things. First, make sure that the action step has become an integral part of the activities of managing and that it will continue. Second, look for additional steps to implement.

The EP process thus has many advantages. The process not only works, but it is easy to implement.

As already noted, there is nothing unnatural about the EP process. What the productivity managers are doing is managing. There is nothing to learn that is completely new, and there are no new and different techniques or concepts to master. There is no large, up-front investment. You must do the first four basic steps, but that is the biggest single commitment. After that, the steps may be small and manageable. And it's possible to measure the results from each manageable step before going on to the next.

Thus no investment is required to implement the EP process of productivity management. There is a modest time cost for doing the first four basic steps. Then you can evaluate the results and *reinvest* a part of the gain from the first four steps in additional productivity action steps.

Many managers are involved when the EP process is implemented. Operating managers proceed in their own units at their own pace. This makes it possible for each organizational unit to move forward with productivity improvement without disrupting operations.

Problems and Issues

A lot of experience has accumulated over the past twenty years with productivity management work. That experience is useful and provides insight into some of the principal problems and issues that you might face while implementing these efforts.

One problem you will surely encounter is that there will be

many levels of interest in and concern about the subject. You will find people who don't care much about productivity improvement.

For many managers, the effectiveness of work is not always a high priority item. They have a list of things to do and projects to accomplish. Improving work effectiveness is not one of those priorities, and when you ask a manager to take on productivity improvement work, you are asking him or her to take time away from other committed projects.

Many managers, including some in high places, will think that productivity is unimportant or low in importance because they are not measured by productivity but by results. That's one reason why it is so important to have productivity measures at every level of the organization.

Many employees and some managers fear productivity improvement. They think that improved productivity might mean losing their jobs or having their status diminished. Even when it is the policy of the company to pay the full cost of productivity improvement, there will be concerns. Unless this issue is addressed up front, productivity improvement will face continuous opposition and many obstacles.

When it is successful, productivity improvement work brings change. Change is always an issue, but productivity improvement often brings about particularly painful changes. The way people work may be inefficient, but they understand that way. The more productive way is an unknown, and some employees might worry about whether they will be successful in doing things the new way.

The changes that go along with productivity improvement work may also mean changes from work that people do well to work they do less well. The changes may mean doing work they don't like to do as much.

Keeping a high level of momentum is always a problem in a major project such as productivity improvement. The bigger the project and the longer it has been running, the harder it is to sustain momentum. Because work is done in manageable parts, one step at a time, it is much easier to maintain momentum under the EP process than it is under any other productivity system.

Every project or special effort has a time to start and a time to finish. You are never finished with productivity management work, but there is a time to stop the special effort, and it's important to know when that is. A project such as productivity management will require the special skill of knowing how to get things done in an organization. In large organizations, this is a very special skill. I never had this type of bureaucratic and relationship skill, so I always looked for people who did. Sooner or later, the development phase would be done, and the administrators would be needed.

Continuing Productivity

Continuing improvement in productivity has become one of the favorite themes of some who work in the field. It makes sense to have a continuous program rather than occasional massive attacks. The problem is that the suggestions for continuous improvement often call for continuing productivity project work and using consultants indefinitely. In the EP process, continuing productivity means building actions into the ongoing management practices.

In my view, there is only one way to build a continuing productivity effort. That way is to build productivity into the management practices of the company. That's why assigning the productivity job to the managers is one of the required action steps in the EP process.

When you consider the recommended action steps, you will see that each is strategic and continuing by design. This system makes productivity management a part of operations.

The most important of the action steps that ensure continuing productivity management is building a productivity culture (see Chapter 3). By nature, that is long term, strategic, and continuing. Providing measures and assigning the job to every manager also provide for continuing efforts in productivity management. Thus three of the four *required* steps in the recommended productivity process are permanent and ongoing activities.

Other action steps have at least elements of continuing productivity improvement. For example, when people become more knowledgeable about utilizing technology for greater work effectiveness, there is an enhanced talent in the organization for the ongoing improvement of productivity. You will also find that at least some parts of empowerment, networking, staffing, manpower management, performance management, and pay for performance are parts of the continuing process and, therefore, contribute to continuing productivity management. EP is a strategic and ongoing method of productivity management that is built into the management practices of the organization.

The recommended productivity management process is a natural part of management. EP is *management* based, so it is possible to make it part of the management process.

Sibson's Fourteen Points on Productivity Management

Certain principles and guidelines are also essential to ensure positive and affirmative productivity action steps and to provide for these actions to become a continuing part of the management process.

W. Edwards Deming and Philip Crosby, who are considered to be leaders in quality management work, summarize their total quality management variations in fourteen points. To help people compare these systems to the EP process, I summarize below my fourteen points that specifically illustrate the guiding principles of EP. These fourteen points are listed roughly from the most important and essential to the important but often optional.

1. The basic job of managing productivity must be assigned to the operating managers. There can be few exceptions to this guideline. One possible exception involves collective bargaining. There may be a separate productivity bargaining group in union relations. There should be no dual organization of any type in productivity work. There cannot be a separate productivity czar or a separate productivity or quality organization. Assign the productivity management job to every operating manager. Give them the authority required to do the job. Give them time to do the job and provide support when they ask for it. Evaluate the

manager's performance in part by how well the productivity management job is done.

2. There must be productivity measures for every unit and division as well as for the company overall. There must also be valid performance appraisal measures of each person's work. You cannot manage productivity unless you measure productivity.

3. There must be a high degree of delegation and empowerment if there is to be ongoing productivity management work that is effective. Participation and involvement are not enough— there must be delegation and empowerment.

4. The employer must pay for the entire human cost of productivity improvement. For example, if greater productivity results in layoffs, the employer must pay the full cost of income lost and any needed retraining and job placement expenses. Consider this a matter of fairness and the cost of getting employees to become full participants in efforts to increase productivity.

5. There must be a well-educated workforce to do the work now and in the foreseeable future. If workers are not sufficiently educated, the company must undertake or support additional education. Provide the education required to be productive in a business area, or get out of that business.

6. There must be a strong performance culture in the firm. Doing one's best must be regarded as the high moral ground by everyone in the organization. Slothfulness, make-work practices, or cheating can never be condoned. This guideline also means that there must be a strong pay for performance culture in the firm. Salary payments should be based only on competitiveness and performance. Wherever there are unit performance measures, there should also be incentive bonus plans. Overall, there should also be success sharing so that all employees share in the success of the company.

7. There must be an inclination and skill in utilizing technology. Machine substitution is not the basic purchasing activity it has been for many years. A great many of the machines that are being substituted for human effort and mental activity are, in fact, at least partly worker controlled. This means that how well workers utilize these machines greatly impacts the resulting productivity.

8. There must be leadership at all levels of management. The leaders themselves must be effective at work, visibly strive for excellence, set high but realistic goals, possess a vision for a better and more productive workplace, and be totally trustworthy. In times of crises, those leaders must take charge and show the way.

9. There must be continuous training, and it must be productivity driven. That training must have a tangible relationship to the effectiveness of work and to the excellence of results. Training must mostly be done by the manager, at the request of the manager, or with the concurrence of the manager. As part of the training environment, the company must encourage initiative and self-development. Recognize that additional education and re-education are also important elements of job training today.

10. The organization must be comfortable with change and capable of quick reaction. There should be intelligence about change, particularly those basic changes impacting both marketing and the operation of the business. Change should be an accepted way of organizational life. However, the company must be *focused* on matters of change; otherwise, the rate and direction of change, and unneeded changes, might actually detract from productivity.

11. There must be equal treatment of every person and at every level of the organization. There can be no preferential treatment for any group, class, or person. This requirement includes executives. You may not be able to achieve perfection in this area because of executive power or compliance matters. But there cannot be preferential treatment and excellence of work.

12. Use management practices and proven business methods in productivity management work. Avoid practices that are unnatural for both the managers and the workers. No strange language should ever be used in productivity management work. Use the dictionary or commonly used business meanings of words. Don't stage productions or playact productivity. Don't celebrate what we should all do anyway.

13. Build a new company loyalty, one that is based on trust, mutual dependency, common goals, and winning team attitudes, not on promises that cannot be kept. Company loyalty isn't dead;

it's just different. The new breed of company loyalty and bonding can be powerful factors in productivity improvement.

14. Build personal values into the company culture. For the employer, this particularly requires a commitment to employee success, assuring all employees a chance to get ahead, candor and forthrightness in all communications, and the proper handling of questions and complaints. Employees must bring honesty, ambition, and a willingness to apply their talents to the best of their ability.

These fourteen principles are very different from those listed for total quality management. EP is a different approach to productivity. I urge you to consider the merits of these principles and to compare them with the fourteen points of Deming and Crosby.

Productivity—The Defining Issue

Productivity will be the defining economic issue for this country and for many businesses in this country for as far into the future as it is possible to see—for the rest of this decade and well into the twenty-first century. Productivity is the defining issue because, more than anything else, it will define the economic conditions of the country in the foreseeable future. Similarly, the effectiveness and excellence of work will determine success or failure for many companies.

Productivity is on the economic center stage because of the special opportunity for improvement by two to three times the rate of improvement that has so far been achieved. A productivity increase of as much as 6 percent per year for twenty years is possible. The economic benefits from such an increase are so enormous that it is worth special consideration by every organization at this time.

This is what can be called the "productivity dividend," the potential economic windfall from extraordinary increases in productivity. The productivity dividend dwarfs the peace dividend of the 1990s. But that productivity dividend must be earned, and so far we have failed to get the productivity increases that are possible.

This country has maintained a competitive advantage in international markets because we had unique technology and higher productivity. It was the high technology and the high productivity that supported our high living standards. Other developed and developing countries are rapidly narrowing our technology advantage and catching up in productivity. We must reverse that narrowing trend and maintain or increase our technology and productivity advantage. That can only be done by a dramatic improvement in education and a substantial increase in productivity. We have it in our grasp to do both of those things right now!

The government can do a great deal to facilitate the achievement of this extraordinary productivity opportunity. Mostly, the government must ensure an even playing field with international competitors. Investment funds must be available, and the government has a big role in making sure that there is investment capital to buy the machines needed to achieve the special productivity opportunity.

I think the government must make sure it doesn't spend the productivity dividend before it is earned in a way that prevents the achievement of productivity improvement. The government must facilitate and not impede this work.

Finally, there isn't any reason why the government can't be more productive in its own operations. The EP process can be effectively used for any government organization. For most government operations, just restructuring, eliminating unproductive practices, and getting rid of excess staff could double productivity.

The center or focal point of productivity work must be each business. Productivity management happens where there is authority for the operation and for the expenditure of capital. Our hope is that business operations of every type and every size set out to increase productivity. Many companies will work to improve productivity if they believe it can be done and know how to do it.

Productivity can be improved everywhere—and improved substantially in most businesses. We know this because of capital substitution possibilities and because many highly visible companies have been doing it. We know how to improve productivity.

The EP process I describe here is by far the best way, and this method is sure to work. But if some other method works for you, use it. We all get dividends from greater productivity.

There are those who will tell you that one of the total quality management methods is the thing to do. Total quality management has received much media coverage, even though only about 2 percent of all companies have used it and more than half of these think it a costly failure. But we should not discourage any method of productivity improvement. Just make sure that it works.

Everyone who reads this book and who is a manager should apply the EP process of productivity management in his or her own area of accountability. Do this whether you are in a big company or a small one. Do this if you are a commercial business or a government department. If you manage an organizational unit, apply these action steps the best you can. Don't wait for the corporation to do it.

My experience with productivity management over the past twenty years has led me to believe that organizations that are most successful in increasing productivity will follow these guidelines:

- First, do the basic action steps extremely well.
- Second, develop superior skills in utilizing technology.
- Third, upgrade the capability of the workforce.
- Fourth, delegate productivity to operating managers throughout the organization and expect those managers to empower employees.
- Fifth, pay for performance.

What is needed is managers who will do these things. There is no master plan that will bring about productivity. There are no panaceas. There are no inspirational messages that will revitalize the economy or any one business. What does it is managing. It is the managers who will, or will not, bring about productivity improvement. It is the managers who will, or will not, do productivity management in a way to exploit this special opportunity to increase productivity at unprecedented rates.

Appendix A

The Sibson Report Productivity Study

Following is a report on recent business experiences and thinking with respect to productivity management. This study covered the experiences and thinking of 227 companies of various sizes and in many different business areas. We focused mostly on companies that have had experience in productivity management or had expressed a special interest in the subject. There was no attempt to get a particular sample because this study was designed to obtain an understanding rather than a count.

Reported here are the principal findings of the study, briefly presented in random order. If you would like more information, please let me know.

1. Somewhat less than two-thirds of all companies in this sample have any productivity data anywhere in the enterprise. Less than half of those with any productivity data have such data in the operations or in organizational units. Many different measures of productivity are used. Every company that has tried to measure productivity has been successful.

We asked why companies did not measure productivity, and most of the answers involved the following:

- It's too costly or difficult.
- It would be divisive or cause trouble.

- Such information isn't practical.
- Productivity can't be measured, or it can't be measured well.
- A good manager can manage productivity without measuring it.

2. I started this study thinking that every company would have a high degree of interest in productivity management, but I found that this was not the case. Here are some of the indications of a torpid attitude toward productivity management in many companies, including many who had done work in productivity management and/or expressed an interest in productivity.

- One-third of all companies don't even keep productivity data.
- Eighty percent of all companies have no mention of productivity goals in their strategic plans.
- About half of all the companies reported that executive interest was lukewarm or inconsistent.
- With respect to productivity management, about half of those agreed that in good years executives have a tendency to say, "Who needs it?" In bad years, those same executives have a tendency to say, "We can't afford it."
- More than half thought that their management had a "this year's" results mentality and that is not supportive of productivity management work.

3. This study suggests that many companies that have organized productivity programs do the work partly to avoid criticism from directors or investors or just because "maybe we should."

4. Many executives think they can purchase productivity and suggest that this is the way to manage productivity. They purchase equipment to increase productivity. The popularity of some of the well-known productivity programs is that there is a belief that you can buy productivity programs as well as productivity equipment.

5. Only about one in four companies studied had adopted any formal productivity program in the past ten years. And this

study was made among companies that had done work in productivity or had expressed an interest in productivity management.

Eighty percent of those who have bought productivity programs report poor or questionable results. Thirty-seven different programs were listed, and I haven't heard of half of them. The most often mentioned programs applied by consultants for this group of companies in the past ten years were quality circles (5 percent of all companies) and total quality management (2 percent of all companies).

6. In this study, which I think is a fair reflection of all business, more than four of five companies have in some way and to a significant degree *empowered* employees. There was widespread thinking that empowerment had a positive impact on productivity. In phone conversations, we verified that the responses reflected a favorable experience with *empowerment*—and not involvement or participation.

7. Not surprisingly, there is broad disagreement about how to increase productivity. Less than one in ten companies think that productivity programs offered by consultants are the way to go. Most managers think that productivity is improved mostly by new plants and equipment. Human resources management professionals emphasize training, team building, management processes, and leadership.

8. In the companies in this study, the average estimate of the potential for productivity improvement is 5.2 percent a year for the next ten years. The actual improvement in these companies in the past ten years was 2.1 percent. Many thought that their companies would do more than twice as well in the future because of the attention given to productivity management and because of new technology.

Keep in mind that this study was among companies having an interest in productivity. Also, past data were factual and future data were predictions.

9. Eighty-five percent of the respondents thought that employees were working at about 75 percent of their potential. About 10 percent thought work was at 90 percent of the potential optimum, and about 5 percent thought work was at 50 percent of

potential. This result is about the same as the opinions expressed by workers in our mainstream survey (see Appendix B).

10. Only about half of all respondents think that employees must be rewarded for improved performance in order to have high productivity. Telephone follow-ups suggest that the response was related to the company's pay system, which was partially or poorly linked to performance.

I think that pay for performance is an essential element of productivity management.

11. Almost every company with a significant part of their workforce belonging to a union has engaged in productivity bargaining. More than 90 percent reported good results. My impression is that companies tend to be more aggressive in removing nonproductive practices in collective bargaining than from nonunion groups of workers.

12. Every enterprise in this study did at least some downsizing in the past ten years, and two-thirds have streamlined their organizations. There was high enthusiasm for these practices as methods of increasing employee productivity.

13. There was little use for and a very low interest in activity value analysis or organizational enrichment.

14. Few companies have done much that is new in the field of scientific management methods and how that might be applied in the technology era to increase productivity. However, there was high interest in the subject, and I received many questions about this.

15. Only about half of all companies have anything in their strategic plans about increasing employee productivity. About half of these have specific productivity objectives in their strategic business plans.

16. Only about one-third of the companies involve human resources management professionals directly and regularly in productivity management work. About one-fourth reported that human resources management professionals were rarely or never involved in such work.

17. Almost all respondents think that resistance to change is a big problem in productivity management. However, it is hard

to get concrete examples of where this has happened or how it happened. This may partly be a case where change is blamed for failures to act affirmatively and effectively.

18. Ninety percent of those surveyed think that people in their company work hard. Slothfulness is rarely thought to be the reason why people are doing less than their best.

19. Most respondents report that EEO has had little impact on productivity, disagreeing with some experts who claim that EEO and affirmative action are responsible for disappointing productivity performance. There is uncertainty about the effect of ADA on productivity but a confidence that it will not significantly cause the hiring of those who are not qualified to do required work in a productive manner.

20. There is widespread agreement that some special interest groups often have the effect of lowering productivity or retarding increases in productivity. Only one company reported cases where special interest groups have caused trouble in the workplace. But all say that the demands of some special interest groups for preferential treatment have caused attitude problems among some constituents, causing a downward pressure on productivity.

21. Whether or not their own company hired consultants for productivity management work, three-fourths of all companies said they thought that consulting work in this area was not very good. The principal complaint was that the consultants wanted to implement canned plans that did not fit the company's requirements or special needs. Most of those we talked to had heard presentations from consultants and thought that although the presentations were good, the professional content was poor.

22. In every conversation with respondents, we asked about the effectiveness ethic. These conversations did indicate that many participants are uncertain or confused about workers' attitudes toward work effectiveness.

23. There was widespread agreement that productivity management is an executive job and that it is a job for the operating managers. But in many specific ways, executives avoid the productivity job, and staff and support people are given authority for productivity work, which at least dilutes managers' account-

ability for productivity management. It is fair to say that account-ability for productivity management is unclear or divided in most of the participating companies, and this is recognized as a problem. For various reasons, however, there is a reluctance to assign the job completely to all operating managers.

24. In both our questionnaire and our conversations, we asked about utilizing the new technologies as a method of increasing productivity. In most cases, the participating companies had done little about this, and in many cases it was a new idea. In this sample, only about 10 percent of the companies had concentrated their attention on this method of increasing productivity.

25. Improved staffing is another major opportunity for increasing productivity. Yet there was little special effort among these companies to increase productivity by better staffing. Most of the participating companies thought they were now doing an excellent job of recruiting.

26. The part of the study that amazed me the most was the answers to questions relating to why workers might not be doing their best. Here is a sample of the responses:

- Ninety percent said their employees are not doing their best because they have to do things the company way. Of course, I asked why this was the case and the answers were mostly vague.
- More than 80 percent said that at least some managers of people won't let the employees do their best. The biggest reason is that the manager is afraid of mistakes. Some are afraid of being embarrassed. I find this hard to believe, but even if it is half right, it is an amazing fact.
- Three-quarters said that their managers won't listen to their employees. Some say that the need to listen to employees better is a reason for participation, but this may be because of a confusion in the meaning of the words "listen" and "hear."
- Not surprisingly, workers are also prevented from doing their best by union make-work rules and because of educational deficiencies.

Appendix B

Mainstream Study

This 1992 survey by the Sibson Reports of a demographic sample of American workers covered sixteen important areas of employee-employer relationships. The three sections that had responses directly related to productivity are reproduced below.

Section 1: The Effectiveness Ethic

1. Do you perform at your reasonable best at work?
   Yes, all the time _39%_   Mostly _48%_   I do what is required _13%_   I do as little as necessary _0%_
2. Are you satisfied with your job
   Yes _63%_   No _8%_   Somewhat _29%_
3. Are you satisfied with your job progress?
   Yes _58%_   No _34%_   ?* _8%_
4. Roughly, would you estimate that people you know work at: 100 percent of their potential _3%_   90 percent of their potential _32%_   75 percent of their potential _53%_   50 percent of their potential _12%_   Less than 50 percent of their potential _0%_
5. Do you think you are being utilized by your employer as well as you should be?   Yes _46%_   No _54%_
6. We have heard a lot about the work ethic; e.g., it is right to

*? means "don't know" or "unsure."

work hard and do your best? Do you think there is a strong work ethic?   Yes _35%_   No _58%_   ? _7%_
7. Do you think you have been properly supervised, trained, and led most of the time at work?
Yes _51%_ No _32%_ ? _2%_ Does not apply to me _15%_
8. Do you think management is effective?
Yes _46%_   No _33%_   ? _21%_
9. Do you know, or do you think you know, ways of doing work more effectively in your company?
Yes _86%_ No _8%_ ? _6%_
10. If there are more effective ways of doing work, why do you think these methods aren't followed? (Check more than one if you wish.)
Unions resist improved methods _3%_   Have to do things the company way _39%_   Managers won't let us _33%_
Managers won't listen _24%_   Other _37%_
11. Do you think that increasing employee productivity is:
Extremely important _63%_ Important _37%_ Not very important _0%_ Unimportant _0%_

Section 7: Pay for Performance

1. Among the different people on a given job, would you generally agree that the better performers should be paid more?   Yes _97%_   No _2%_   ? _1%_
2. Do you think it's practical to rate performance from the best to the worst?   Yes _70%_   No _17%_   ? _13%_
3. For people whose work you know, could you judge how effective they are if you used five different levels?
Yes _59%_   No _19%_   ? _22%_
4. Do you think length of service should be considered in pay even though it isn't reflected in performance?
Yes _33%_   No _59%_   ? _8%_
5. Should a worker's need for money affect pay (e.g., should a person with five children get more than a person with one child)?   Yes _2%_   No _97%_   ? _1%_
6. Should age be a factor in pay unrelated to performance?
Yes _1%_   No _97%_   ? _2%_

7. Assume that Mary is 50 percent more productive than Frank. Should Mary get something like 50 percent more money than Frank? Yes _27%_ No _50%_ ? _23%_
8. Should race, religion, sex, or national origin ever be a consideration in pay matters? Yes _0%_ No _99%_ ? _1%_
9. Should a person who is believed to have great future potential have that considered even if it doesn't show in his or her current performance? Yes _25%_ No _63%_ ? _12%_

Section 10: Unions

1. Do you think unions have been helpful to working people in the past? Yes _70%_ No _15%_ ? _15%_
2. Generally, do you favor and support unions in the United States today? Yes _44%_ No _46%_ ? _10%_
3. Do you think that union demands have caused jobs to be lost overseas because of high pay costs and low productivity? Yes _76%_ No _6%_ ? _18%_
4. Do you think unions should support efforts to increase productivity? Yes _98%_ No _0%_ ? _2%_
5. Should unions in companies that provide essential services (hospitals, schools, public transportation, etc.) be permitted to strike? Yes _18%_ No _75%_ ? _7%_
6. Do you think unions should be involved in politics? Yes _15%_ No _75%_ ? _10%_
7. Do you think secondary strikes are okay (e.g., a strike against a company with which the union has no disagreement in order to get at another company that the union does have a dispute with)? Yes _3%_ No _90%_ ? _7%_
8. Some people think that unions are not always responsible in their actions; e.g., would you have supported the union during the air traffic controllers' strike? Yes _11%_ No _78%_ ? _11%_
9. Some workers think that union dues are too expensive. Do you agree? Yes _81%_ No _15%_ ? _4%_
10. Some workers think that unions have lost touch with working people. Do you agree? Yes _83%_ No _9%_ ? _8%_

Index